DO YOUR KIDS
KNOW
YOU LOVE THEM?

DO YOUR KIDS KNOW YOU LOVE THEM?

Fred Streit, Ed.D. and
Beatrice Krauss, Ph.D.

KENSINGTON BOOKS
http://www.kensingtonbooks.com

KENSINGTON BOOKS are published by

Kensington Publishing Corp.
850 Third Avenue
New York, NY 10022

ISBN 1-57566-547-6
Kensington and the K logo Reg. U.S. Pat. & TM Off.

First Kensington Paperback Printing: September, 2000
10 9 8 7 6 5 4 3 2 1

Printed in the United States of America

CONTENTS

INTRODUCTION

For many years, I have been aware of the immense importance of the perception of love from another person as a stabilizing and positive influence in our lives. My research had reconfirmed the anecdotal evidence and the widely held intuitive beliefs of many people. My goal was to find ways to make positive change in families' lives by enhancing the perception of love. I already knew that it worked in my own family. I had been told many times by strangers that these concepts had changed their lives. More recently, one of my colleagues has been teaching pastoral counselors to use the concepts and methods contained in this book to help families. Not only have they been able to use the training and concepts to help others, but they are reporting that their lives have been positively changed, as well.

I am most grateful to Steve Zacharius, president of Kensington Books, for his belief in this book and his support. Executive Editor Tracy Bernstein and Editor Amy Garvey have added much to the clarity and strength of this book. Rachel Faugno has displayed her fantastic skill at reworking my scientific prose into readable, comprehensible English. She has moved the art of clear communication to a new, superior level.

My children—David, Paul, and Joan—and my wife, Janet, are the true creators of this book. Throughout their lives, I have been aware of the importance of having the children perceive my love and have tried very hard to make it so. Seeing the kind of parents they have become leads me to believe that Jan and I have succeeded. I love all of them and the seven grandchildren very much and I work at making sure they perceive that love.

Fred Streit, Ed.D.

As with most mothers, I am a collector . . . of the drawings and cards that date back to my children's infancy: Mother's Day and Valentine cards, hand drawn, with the straightforward expressions of affection of unsophisticated youth. Seldom do we receive such clear messages: a heart held out in a hand, "I love you" in block letters. In fact, one psychological researcher has referred to the majority of the finely articulated adult expressions of emotion—the lump in the throat, the half-smile—as "choked off" or partially expressed emotion. This book asks that we give back to our children, in a form that they easily perceive, some of that unself-conscious love, admiration, and pride. I wish to thank my family, for they make it so easy to be proud and loving: my sons, Michael and Daniel; Michael's wife, Susan; my two grandchildren, Ethan and Gabriel; and my loving husband, Herb. I also wish to acknowledge all those good people who act as parenting models for the rest of us, giving their children skills, hope, and the gregarious warmth that comes from being loved.

Beatrice Krauss, Ph.D.

DO YOUR KIDS
KNOW
YOU LOVE THEM?

CHAPTER 1

DO <u>YOUR</u> KIDS KNOW YOU LOVE THEM?

Do you love your children?

If you're like most parents, your answer is probably a resounding "Yes. Of course I do!"

For most of us there is no other emotion that quite matches that intense and complicated mixture of pride, protectiveness, and connection that we feel toward our children. (Which is not to say that we don't occasionally feel some equally intense but much less positive emotions toward them.) Our children are a part of us, and our love for them is as evident to them as the fact that the Earth is round. Right?

Well, not quite.

You see, our children are not mind-readers, and neither are we. What we feel and what they *believe* we feel are sometimes two very different things.

This became perfectly clear in the case of a couple we know (we'll call them Ann and Bob) who had two sons and, after a wait of several years, a much-longed-for daughter.

Ann and Bob made it clear to their sons that they expected them to achieve to the best of their abilities. They kept up the pressure to achieve, including minimizing the opportunity for the boys to participate in sports and extracurricular activities. As a result, the boys did quite well in school and went on to attend prestigious colleges.

The couple tended to be more indulgent toward their daughter and encouraged her to enjoy herself. When this highly intelligent girl barely graduated from high school and then flunked out of junior college, Ann and Bob were stunned. They asked her why she had failed.

"You thought they were smarter, so you really pushed my brothers, but I could tell you didn't think I was smart enough to make it," she responded. "That's probably why you love them more than you do me."

Ann and Bob were horrified to learn that their beloved daughter felt that way—that what she perceived was so very different from what they felt toward her. It took a lot of discussion and hard work, including changing some of their own behaviors, before their daughter was able to perceive the deep love that her parents felt for her. As you will learn later in this book, her perception of what her parents expected of her affected what she expected of herself. She had an "imagined expectation" which was far lower than her parents' real expectation.

How do children know they are loved?

We've all heard the phrase "Love is an action verb." Nowhere is that claim more true than in our relationship with our children. Very young children, especially, interpret love as "What have you done for me?" When we feed and bathe and read to and play with and comfort our toddlers, they interpret all of that care-giving as love. Loving is *doing*.

Around the age of eight, though, things begin to get complicated. The way that children perceive their world slowly changes. They no longer exist in the simple black-and-white world of early childhood but instead begin to detect shades of gray. Things that once were one-dimensional develop depth and hidden meanings. Children's old concrete ways of looking at things become confused by the onset of abstract thought.

When Mommy leaves the room, a very young child is convinced that she is gone forever. Not quite "out of sight, out of mind" but more "out of sight, gone." The child finds it hard to understand that Mommy can be someplace the child can't see. Abstract-thinking ability enables children to comprehend that things can exist beyond their immediate tangible surrounding. They begin to understand that there is a reality that may not be visible to them.

Now, the capacity for abstract thinking is one of mankind's great strengths. It is what has enabled us to build skyscrapers and write great books and compose music and put a man on the moon. But it can change our relationships as we become aware that things are not necessarily what they appear to be. We look for hidden meanings behind a compliment or a casual remark. We assign positive or negative motives to the behavior of others. We interpret situations by paying attention to some information, modifying another part, and ignoring the rest. In short, we create our own reality and then test it.

As human beings, our interpretation of events and actions—that is, our _perception_ of reality—is reality itself to us.

The development of abstract thinking is a normal, healthy part of growing up. But it presents new challenges for parents. We can no longer go about the business of parenting in the old ways and assume that our children will view our actions as love. As our children grow into adolescence, they put their own spin on our behavior. They look behind the obvious for secret motives and hidden agendas. In effect, it is their interpretation of our actions—_their perception of reality_—that determines whether or not they feel loved.

Thus, it is not only what we do but how the children see it that determines what they believe is true. Their spin on what we do is determined by what we actually do, their stage of development, their previous experiences, and their personalities.

What happens when children don't feel loved?

All human beings need love. We all need closeness and support and appreciation for our own special qualities. Babies who are not given warmth and closeness may suffer from a tragic malady known as "failure to thrive." There is evidence that children in foundling homes have died from a lack of love. Children and adolescents who do not feel loved may respond to their situation in angry, confrontational, or self-destructive ways. Further, the effects of not feeling loved as a child may last a lifetime. One Harvard study, begun just after World War II, followed the lives of young men for thirty-five years. Those who reported that they hadn't felt loved as a child suffered a much higher incidence of heart disease, high blood pressure, and other physical ailments.* This was true whether the parent in question was the mother or the father. The men who felt love from their parents experienced about half the incidence of physical ailments as did their non-loved peers.

Several years ago, Dr. Streit conducted a study in eastern Pennsylvania in which 6,000 teenagers anonymously answered 105 questions. Along with questions about school attitudes, drug and alcohol use, sexuality, church attendance, and peer influence, he asked, "How would you describe your family?"

The response choices were: very close; somewhat close; not too close; not close at all. A full twenty percent of the children expressed the belief that their family was not close at all. These same children reported that they:

- were not happy most of the time;
- felt life was boring;
- liked to do things to shock people;
- felt they had less fun than most people;
- seldom felt close to people;
- felt they couldn't control their lives;
- didn't care about their grades in school;
- didn't expect to go to college;
- went along with peer groups to use drugs and alcohol.

Many studies conducted by other researchers support these results. What kids seem to be telling us is that if they don't feel close to their families—if they don't feel loved—they are likely to have a hard time fitting into society.

Even those kids who seem to adapt to their (perceived) unloving environment may suffer serious damage to their self-esteem. Around the time children develop the capacity for abstract thinking, they begin to acquire a heightened sense of their own identity. They may see themselves as someone who is a good student, or a troublemaker, or a popular kid, or an outcast, or. . . . You fill in the blanks. Peers, teachers, and others in their expanding social circle contribute to this self-image. But the most important influence on how children see themselves, on how they evaluate their own self-worth, is how they believe their parents feel about them.

You can help your children feel loved.

A few years ago, a man stood up during one of our presentations and said, "It's hard enough being a parent in today's world without having to second-guess how our kids are interpreting our actions. Why isn't it enough to love them and do our best and leave it at that? After all, that's the way most of us were raised and we turned out all right."

He had a point, of course. It's arguable that our parents didn't have to work so hard at maintaining a close family because families were naturally closer back then. There were fewer divorces. Fewer single-parent households. Fewer outside negative pressures on kids. More relatives around to help knit the family together. (It also can be argued that many things look better in retrospect!)

Regardless of how things were in the past, most people would agree that parents today face enormous pressures. In the so-called Communication Age, communication among family members too often breaks down. Love and good intentions get misinterpreted or ignored, and frustration and alienation too often result.

Traditional wisdom would have us treat the *children* when

family problems arise. After all, if the parents are giving love and the kids are acting up, the kids must need therapy or some other intervention to get straightened out. We assume that once they realize that they have misunderstood things, that they have misinterpreted their parents' actions, everything will be okay.

We don't agree. Our belief is that the best way to change family relationships is *to work with the parents*, to help them learn to show love in ways that are meaningful and important to their children. If children do not feel loved, the most effective way to treat the problem is *to change the parental behaviors that led to that false perception*. To deal with major problems probably requires acquiring new methods to show love. Minor problems appear only to need a "tweak" of old behaviors.

This doesn't mean that the job of parenting just got harder. Just the opposite. By incorporating the skills and tools presented in this book, the job of parenting may grow progressively easier. You'll stop expending energy where it doesn't pay off and put it where it will do the most good. You'll learn how to avoid making painful mistakes and how to communicate more effectively with your child.

In the process you will become a better parent. Your relationship with your children will improve. And you will be well on your way to helping them become the responsible, competent adults you want them to be. In the pages that follow, we'll show you how.

---

* Russek, G. & Schwartz, G. "Feelings of parental caring predict health status in midlife: a 35 year follow-up of the Harvard Mastery of Stress Study." *Journal of Behavioral Medicine* 1997 Feb; 20(1) 1-13.

CHAPTER 2

PUTTING LOVE IN THE BANK

Is love really important?

We were on our way to having lunch with a colleague when we became aware of what we were hearing on the radio. Song after song told of lost love, unrequited love, wonderful love, puppy love, fading love, and newfound love. Commercials told the listener which products to use to be more lovable and how to attract love. It sounded as if love could solve everything, and what it couldn't solve wasn't worth having. Interestingly, all of the songs of love had to do with couples—none had anything to do with parents and children.

We talked about it over lunch with a young colleague, a single mother who remarked, "I guess if people believe that love makes the world go round, then we don't have to do anything with kids but love them."

It would be nice if it were as simple as that, but of course it isn't. One difficulty, as we stated earlier, lies in the fact that children may not perceive our love for them. (Much more on this later.) Another difficulty lies in the question of how we define "love." That overused word can mean any number of things depending on whom you ask. We told our colleague that by our definition, love is a deep feeling of caring, expressed through a consistent pattern of behaviors that will promote the child's growth and development as a well-adjusted individual.

She sat back in her chair, a frown of concentration wrinkling her brow. "Wow!" she said after a moment. "That's a pretty tall order. You mean every time I discipline my son or tell him what he can or can't do, I'm going to stunt his emotional growth or something? Are you saying that I shouldn't discipline my son?"

We assured her that an important part of loving children is providing structure and control in their lives—a form of consistency. Gushing permissiveness without establishing limits only teaches that there are no limits to normal behavior—hardly a way to live with anyone, let alone a maturing child.

What's more, there is no such thing as a "perfect" parent. Everyone has bad days when it's hard to *feel* love, much less *show* it. Maybe your job pressures hit an all-time high, or your car broke down, or you're coming down with the flu. Maybe your children just washed your entire CD collection in the bathtub. Maybe you just want to be left alone.

It's okay. Nobody can be expected to show love all the time.

If you consider showing and perceiving love as being similar to making cash deposits in a savings account over time, it is likely that a considerable positive balance has already accrued. As with money, it's possible to make a withdrawal on a "rainy day" without sacrificing the principal or closing the account. As long as you put in more than you take out, you should be fine.

"Whew!" our young colleague exclaimed. "That's a relief. But I think I'll start a systematic savings plan by making sure I know a lot more about showing and perceiving love. That way, I know I'll always be putting in more than I'll need for that rainy day."

We said that was an excellent idea. In fact, it would be a very good thing if all parents paid closer attention to their "love deposits," because studies have supported what common sense suggests: Children who do not feel loved often suffer in their social, academic, and emotional development.

It is the showing and perceiving of love that is the insulator against future problems for children. Later in this book we will show the link between perceiving love and a host of problem behaviors in children.

How does love help children develop a positive self-image?

One of children's developmental tasks is to establish an identity that is separate from their parents. Children as young as two are engaged in trying to establish a sense of selfhood (thus, the "terrible twos"). At this age and for several years to come, children perceive love on a concrete level. That is, they take things at face value. If parents are nurturing and responsive to the child's needs, the child feels loved. Feeling loved helps the child feel *valued*, leading to a positive self-image. There is some value in feeling that you are the center of your parents' universe—at least when you're quite young.

By around age ten, however, most children begin to develop the capacity for abstract thinking. That is, they become aware that the world around them is multilayered, and that human interactions are quite complex. They begin to evaluate events and people (including their parents) in a new way, trying to see behind the obvious to glean any hidden meanings. They question and test whether an eight o'clock bedtime is for their benefit or to create free time for their parents, or whether there's any merit to having to wash their hands before dinner. The favorite question is "why?"

If you observe children, you will see that they spend a certain amount of time playacting—before mirrors and before adults. Through the reflections in the mirrors and by the reactions of adults, children learn more about who they are and what "others" may see in them. If the parents show love—*and if the children see and feel that love*—things are positive. Over time, the children feel valued and develop a positive self-image.

During the past twenty years, increased attention has been paid to the problems of children of alcoholic and other addicted parents. Most addicted parents have little energy to devote to finding ways to show their children love. As a result, many of these unfortunate children blame themselves for their parents' addiction. Often they develop fantasies about the family relationships, which they tell to others as truth and begin to believe themselves.

According to the research, in the absence of perceived love from their parents, these children of addicted parents develop patterns of poor self-concepts masked with tales of fantasy of idyllic family life, and impaired abilities to develop solid interpersonal relationships.

But even in households where no addiction is present, where, in fact, family life seems "normal," children may suffer from the perception that their parents don't love them. Once they begin to *perceive* that their parents don't love or value them (regardless of the reality), their fragile sense of selfhood becomes damaged. They may reason, "If my parents don't love me, then I must not be lovable. I must not be of value." Their self-image suffers.

Is there a connection between not perceiving love and having physical and social problems?

Health practitioners have long known about the connection between body and mind. Studies that show how laughter prolongs life are no longer hot news. Demonstrations of how the caring behavior of nurses reduces surgical trauma have wrought changes in many hospital practices. And a thirty-five-year follow-up study of Harvard undergraduates revealed that ninety percent of young men who reported not having a warm relationship with their mothers during childhood developed one or more of the following stress-related diseases at mid-life: coronary artery disease, high blood pressure, ulcers, and alcoholism. Among those who described their relationship with their mothers as "warm" (we might call it a perception of being loved), the incidence of these diseases was less than half—forty-five percent.

Likewise, research has shown an important relationship between how people perceive things and what they do. Our work over the course of many years has focused on finding solutions to the problems of substance abuse, including alcoholism, HIV/AIDS transmission, and other related health and social problems, particularly among adolescents. We knew from our previous work that family closeness was related to problems, and that perception of parents was related to family closeness.

In one study we asked teens to rate their family's closeness, to report how they believed their parents treated them, and if and how these teens were using drugs. The results showed that the child's perception of parental behavior correlated to the use of different drugs. Although the equations and explanations are very complex, we show them in a general way on this circle.

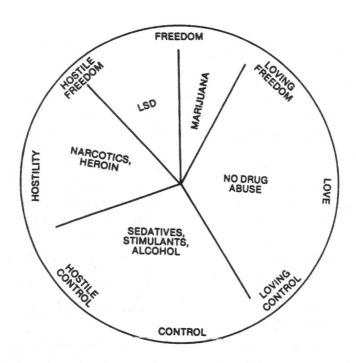

Every child generally perceives a little bit of each and every one of the parenting styles shown in the circle, with certain characteristics being dominant. While it is tempting to say that the lack of love from parents *causes* drug abuse, we can't prove it. However, children's perceptions of love are clearly related to these problems. Teens who reported that they perceived love from their parents were much less likely to abuse drugs.

What was more surprising was that our studies suggested a correlation between parenting *style* and drug of choice (see Chapter 3 for more on parenting styles). For example, parental behavior that was viewed as hostile was associated with heroin use, whereas too much freedom was associated with the use of marijuana.

Of course, we are not claiming that drug abuse can be explained as easily as the diagram might indicate. This circle should not be used as an easy predictor of who will use drugs. Many, many factors affect children's decisions to use or not use these substances. Perception of parental behavior is only one of those factors. But our studies indicate it is a crucial one.

Our research also suggests a correlation between feeling unloved and criminal behavior. For a year, every child remanded to an unidentified juvenile detention home completed our "Perception of Parental Behavior" questionnaire. The purpose was to provide the counselors with some insight into the children's perceived home situations, resulting in a more accurate, more sensitive treatment process.

Analysis of the information revealed that the child's perception of parent behavior was highly related to the type of crime committed. Those children who perceived a harsh, hostile, controlling environment from their parents tended to commit crimes against people. Those who perceived an overly structured and controlling environment, but without the rejection and hostility, tended to commit property crimes. None of the children in the detention home reported perceiving their parents as exhibiting a great deal of love and caring.

In another study, school children completed the "Perception of Parental Behavior" questionnaire regarding their parents and (in a modified version) their classroom teachers. The results showed that the children's classroom behavior was related to their perceptions of *their parents* rather than to their perception of *their teacher.* Obviously, this cannot mean that what a teacher does in the classroom has no effect on a child's classroom behavior. It does mean that the perception of parents' actions is a major factor in classroom behavior and that the perception of the teacher plays a lesser but apparently important role.

Our purpose in citing these studies is not to suggest that every child who feels unloved will abuse drugs, become a criminal, or have a terrible life. Such a claim would be ludicrous and cannot be supported. We regularly hear of celebrities and other notables who came from love-deprived backgrounds (as they perceived it) and nevertheless succeed in almost all areas of life. An enormously popular TV talk show hostess has been widely quoted as saying, "I was never, ever loved." A former president of the United States has said, "Whatever happened, I knew that I was loved." Certainly there are people as well who know they are loved but choose to do things that defy explanation.

Our wish is simply to emphasize that there is a correlation between what children perceive and what they do. We know that if children perceive love from their parents, it is far less likely that they will develop significant behavioral problems.

A Case Study

Beth's family had been living in the neighborhood for about two years when Sharon's parents bought a house down the street. Each girl had two older brothers and parents who were college graduates with professional careers. Throughout middle and high school, the girls were friends, sharing similar goals and scholastic abilities.

Although both sets of parents took an active interest in their daughters' lives, there were some differences in their parenting styles. Beth's family was very competitive. Beth's father undertook and completed many of her school projects for her—assuring good grades. Her mother took pains to involve Beth in appropriate social situations where she could meet the "right" boys and achieve social mobility.

Sharon's parents provided structure, control, and much supportive love, but they didn't do her work for her. They counseled against some unwise social settings, but they encouraged her decision-making and self-reliance.

After graduating from college, Beth had difficulty accomplishing much in a career on her own but experimented socially with three engagements to be married. She married, had two children, and then divorced and returned to live with her parents. Sharon was far more successful in her career, which she continued while married and raising three children. She recently said to her parents, "You know, I had a great childhood. I always knew I was loved."

Did Sharon's perception of being loved contribute to her success? We believe so. On the other hand, are Beth's difficulties related to a perception of not having been loved? Again, we believe it is likely.

This is not to say that Beth's parents loved her any less than Sharon's parents loved their daughter. There is no way to gauge or compare the degree of human love, and it is useless to try. Suffice it to say that Beth's parents' way of expressing love—that is, their *behavior*—may have told Beth that while they loved her, they did not think very highly of her capabilities. She may have perceived that their love was conditional, linked to the premise that she was not as capable as they would like her to be.

In the long run, it is not how much love parents feel that makes the difference—it is the quantity and quality of love children perceive. In the following chapters, we will see how parent behavior contributes to children's perception of love.

CHAPTER 3

WHAT'S YOUR COMMUNICATION STYLE?

What's your parenting style?

In the first two chapters we've stated that although you no doubt love your children very deeply, it's your children's *perception* of being loved that is crucial to their well-being. There may be a very big difference between what you feel toward them and what they believe they see you doing.

While we as parents are accustomed to observing and evaluating our children's actions, we may not be aware that our children are simultaneously observing and evaluating our actions toward them.

Of course, much of their evaluation takes place on a subconscious level. They are not consciously examining every word and action of their parents. (Who could withstand such scrutiny?) Instead, it is within the context of our daily interactions with our children that they perceive dozens of messages about our attitudes toward them. Are we caring or distant, trusting or suspicious, loving or indifferent? Do we view them as worthwhile individuals or as troublesome annoyances?

Their answers to these and hundreds of similar questions are determined to a great extent by how we behave toward them. In other words, their interpretation of our behavior— that is, *their perception of our feelings toward them*—has a powerful impact on how much love they perceive from us.

One of the most fundamental behaviors they respond to is our parenting style.

Through much research, we have identified twenty-six distinct styles of discipline, encouragement, and reaction. These vary not only in what parents *do* but in the amount of *focus* on the child—from ignoring them to overinvolvement. Here is a brief description of each of the styles:

1. *Extreme Freedom*–A complete absence of control over the behavior of the children. The child operates in a world of family anarchy.
2. *Lax Discipline*–Parents can't and don't refuse any of the child's wishes. In addition, the parents don't enforce any discipline or structure on the child.
3. *Moderate Freedom*–Parents put some limits and controls on the child's behavior.
4. *Encouraging Sociability*–Parents encourage the child's social interactions with people of all ages.
5. *Encouraging Independent Thinking*–Parents encourage the child's decision-making, creativity, and independent activity.
6. *Equal Treatment*–Parents attempt to treat the child as an equal in areas depending on the age and maturity of the child.
7. *Positive Evaluation*–Parents tell the child about the "good" things he/she does and reinforce positive behaviors.
8. *Sharing*–Parents like to be with the child, do things together, and talk with the child.
9. *Expressing Affection*–Parents express affection to the child both verbally and physically.
10. *Emotional Support*–Parents help the child feel better when the child is sad, afraid, or unhappy.
11. *Intellectual Stimulation*–Parents work at getting the child to think and to enjoy learning.
12. *Being Child-Centered*–Parents make the child feel that he/she is very important in the lives of the family, and in particular in the lives of the parents.

13. *Possessiveness*–Parents don't seem to want the child to grow up, and they fear that the child will move away from them both physically and emotionally.
14. *Protectiveness*–Parents appear to worry about the child's welfare almost all of the time.
15. *Intrusiveness*–Parents insist on knowing everything going on in the child's life, particularly when they are not with the child.
16. *Suppressing Aggression*–Parents prohibit the child from showing anger or displeasure at them or at other people.
17. *Control Through Guilt*–Parents use guilt as a method of control to get the child to do as they wish.
18. *Direction*–Parents make the decisions for the child without consulting with the child.
19. *Strictness*–Parents make and enforce many rules covering *all* aspects of the child's life.
20. *Punishment*–Infractions of rules by the child are dealt with very quickly and often with undue punishment.
21. *Nagging*–Parents enforce their wishes by giving the child little peace until the child does their bidding.
22. *Negative Evaluation*–Parents focus on telling the child about the "bad" things he/she does.
23. *Irritability*–Parents lose their tempers and easily become quite angry with the child.
24. *Rejection*–Parents make the child feel unwanted and unloved.
25. *Neglect*–Parents seem to be unaware of the child's needs.
26. *Ignoring*–Parents spend little time with the child and share few activities with him/her.

While we can identify twenty-six parenting styles that seem to be independent of each other, they actually overlap. For example, extreme levels of *irritability* "slide" into preliminary forms of *rejection*. Extreme *rejection* "slides" into *neglect* and so on. Conceptually, the twenty-six styles can be clustered into eight groups and then form a continuous circle.

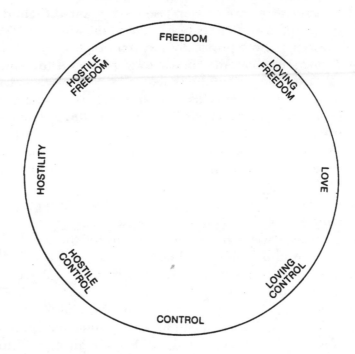

The eight clusters and the styles contained in each cluster are as follows:

- **Love** positive evaluation, sharing, expressing affection, emotional support.
- **Loving Control** intellectual stimulation, child-centered, possessive, protective.
- **Control** intrusive, suppression of aggression, control through guilt, parental direction.
- **Hostile Control** strictness, punishment, nagging.
- **Hostility** irritability, negative evaluation, rejection.
- **Hostile Freedom** neglect, ignoring.
- **Freedom** extreme freedom, lax discipline.
- **Loving Freedom** moderate freedom, encouraging sociability, encouraging independent thinking, equal treatment.

These parenting styles should not be viewed as rigidly exclusive of one another. Most of us have a dominant style that blends somewhat with other styles, depending on the circumstances. What is important as you begin to explore how children perceive love is for you to raise your awareness of your own behavior: Which of these parenting styles do you think best describes you? Think of different circumstances with your children. In each circumstance, which parenting style do you think best describes what you do? More important, which style do your *children* think best describes you? For most parents, the styles will vary based on the situation.

Why won't you listen to me?

Sound familiar? This complaint is heard all too often from parents *and* children who are frustrated by their inability to get through to one another. Both feel as if they are hitting their heads against a brick wall. Both feel as though the other person is just too stubborn to listen. Both experience a sense of rejection that can quickly escalate into anger.

The inability to communicate clearly with each other is one of the most vexing problems between parents and their children, particularly adolescent children. Sometimes it almost seems as if everyone is speaking a different language. In some ways, they are.

Can you imagine calling your son or daughter by using a dog whistle? It makes little sense to call another person using a whistle that makes sounds beyond the range of their hearing. It can't work, simply because the other person cannot hear the signal.

Or imagine being asked for directions by foreign tourists on the streets of New York City. Frustrated that we don't speak their language we find ourselves speaking louder and louder, as if the increased volume could help their understanding. Of course it doesn't work, and we've wondered at times if there are tourists who still wander the streets of New York hopelessly lost because of our inability to communicate in the appropriate language.

If you're like most parents, you have probably had the feeling that you are speaking a language your child simply cannot hear (regardless of the volume) or doesn't understand. One reason for this may be that you don't communicate on the same wavelength.

Just as you have a certain parenting style (or styles) that you use most frequently, you also have a communication style that affects the way you interact with your children.

Each of us understands and communicates with the world mostly through a combination of three senses: sight (visual), hearing (auditory), and feelings (intuition). One of these senses is usually dominant over the others.

For example, an auditory person prefers to hear spoken words for the information needed to describe thoughts or actions. A visual person uses sight images in remembering and thinking. A feeling person depends more on intuition and gut feelings to sense things. Everyone uses all of the senses, although we tend to be dominant in one of the three. In fact, the term "common sense" originated with Aristotle and meant using all of our senses to understand the world.

None of these modalities is better than any of the others as a way of communicating with and understanding the world. We are all entitled to our own way of perceiving and interacting with others. However, if we wish to be effective in communicating with our children, we need to know which sense they use most of the time in dealing with their world. If we can communicate with them through their dominant sense, we have a far better chance of being understood. If we are understood, we can be perceived as showing love. By *listening to* and *watching* our children we can see if they understood what was conveyed to them.

We once accompanied a class of children to a natural history museum. Standing in front of a forest tableau, one of the children asked, "Is that a real bear?" The guide carefully explained that it once was and then explained the practice of taxidermy and carefully noted that it was now a stuffed bear.

Later, in front of a tableau of explorers, the child asked if the explorer Cabezon was a real person. The reply was "Yes." Later the child wrote in an essay, "What I liked best about the trip was the stuffed people."

What was said and what the child heard were clearly two different things!

What's your communication style?

People whose visual sense is dominant might describe the world using words such as: *It appears to me. I drew a blank. I need to get clear on this picture. I plan to scrutinize the image and see if I can change my outlook. We need a more colorful perspective.*

Other sight or visual words include: *brighten, examine, foresee, glow, hindsight, insight, inspect, illuminate, mirror, notice, obscure, obvious, reflect.*

More visual words: *appears to me, bird's-eye view, clear cut, take a dim view of, beyond a shadow of a doubt, horse of a different color, seeing eye to eye, hazy idea, make a scene, look the other way, take a peek, in the mind's eye, pretty as a picture, tunnel vision.*

Those whose auditory sense is dominant might use the following words to describe their world: *That rings a bell. I hear you. Sounds good to me. Listen to this. Don't tune me out. I asked myself.*

Other auditory words include: *announce, earshot, discuss, gossip, hear, hush, listen, loud, mention, noise, oral, pronounce, remark, report, rhyme, ring, roar, rumor, say, shrill, squeak, speechless, talk.*

More auditory words: *be in harmony, blabbermouth, clear as a bell, earful, fevered pitch, lend me your ear, hidden message, hold your tongue, idle talk, it's a snap, tattletale, tuned in, tuned out, turn a deaf ear, voice an opinion, word for word.*

People whose sense of intuition is dominant might use the following words to describe their world: *callous, concrete, crushed, emotional, feel, firm, flow, grasp, handling, hassle, heated, hit, hold, hustle, lukewarm, motion, panic, pressure, relieve, softly.*

Other intuitive words: *All washed up. Be on your toes. Chip off the old block. Come to grips with it. Cool, calm, and collected. Get a handle on it. Hand in hand. Lay your cards on the table. Let it sink in. One step at a time. On the right track. Start from scratch. Stiff upper lip. Tickles my fancy.*

Here is a simple, brief test to help you discover your dominant sense. You will be doing this test twice—once to discover the sense in which you are dominant, and then to find the sense in which your child is dominant. Children over ten can complete the test themselves. We suggest that you make two copies of the test so that both your child and your partner might also complete it.

Instructions: Read each pair of sentences carefully. Decide which of the two is closer in describing what you'd rather do, enjoy doing more, are happier at, or find easier to do. Select the letter for your answer and then circle that letter. *If you are completing the survey for your child, put yourself in your child's shoes and answer as if you were your son or daughter.* **Do not discuss your answers with anyone while you are completing this test.**

Question	Circle letter
1. Is it easier to remember . . . **V** who has the darkest color hair in your family? **A** who speaks the softest in your family?	**V A**
2. Would you rather . . . **A** hear your favorite singer? **F** relax at your favorite spot?	**A F**
3. Is it easier to remember . . . **V** the color and shape of the entrance to your neighbor's house? **A** whether a pair of shoes squeak?	**V A**
4. Would you prefer to . . . **V** imagine going to a new place? **F** jump into a cold pool or shower?	**V F**

5. Can you . . .   **A F**
   A hum a few bars of a tune?
   F remember the warmth of the sun on
      a beach?

6. Is it easier to . . .   **V A**
   V add 234 and 127 in your head?
   A recognize the difference between a police
      and an ambulance siren?

7. Do you prefer . . .   **A F**
   A having someone tell you what happened?
   F experiencing what happens?

8. Is it easier for you . . .   **V A**
   V to see through an insecure person?
   A to listen to an inner voice about a person?

9. Are you better at . . .   **V A**
   V keeping a sharp eye out?
   A keeping an ear to the ground?

10. Do you enjoy . . .   **V F**
    V seeing eye to eye with other people?
    F meeting on common ground?

11. Do you prefer to . . .   **V A**
    V see the whole picture before the details?
    A think before you speak?

12. Are you more comfortable with . . .   **V F**
    V a bright idea?
    F a gut feeling?

13. When it's easy to do . . .   **A F**
    A it's a snap.
    F it's smooth sailing.

14. When other people are wrong . . .   **A   F**
    A they're barking up the wrong tree.
    F they're headed in the wrong direction.

15. You learn something by . . .   **V   F**
    V seeing the light?
    F allowing it to sink in?

16. A good idea . . .   **V   F**
    V brightens your outlook?
    F tickles your fancy?

17. That's not what I meant to say because . . .   **V   A**
    V that's a horse of a different color.
    A that's not what I said.

18. You don't understand . . .   **A   F**
    A because you didn't hear what I said.
    F and you're way off base.

19. Are you better at . . .   **V   F**
    V keeping a sharp eye out?
    F playing your hunches?

20. Do you prefer to . . .   **A   F**
    A hear what a person has to say?
    F meet him on common ground?

21. Are things better for you . . .   **V   A**
    V when you see eye to eye?
    A when you feel tuned into someone?

22. Are you better at . . .   **V   F**
    V keeping a sharp eye out?
    F being on your toes?

23. When you recognize something . . .   **V   A**
    V it stirs an image?
    A it rings a bell?

24. When it happened . . .   **V**   **F**
    V your mind went blank?
    F you felt numb?

25. When it happened a second time . . .   **A**   **F**
    A you were dumbfounded?
    F you went numb?

26. You handle an insult by . . .   **V**   **A**
    V overlooking it?
    A tuning it out?

27. People who ignore my needs are . . .   **V**   **F**
    V blind?
    F unfeeling?

28. When things go right, I have a sense of . . .   **A**   **F**
    A harmony?
    F tranquillity?

29. When I'm really tired . . .   **A**   **F**
    A I'm flat.
    F I'm at peace.

30. A really fine painting seems to . . .   **V**   **F**
    V show a special quality.
    F send off special vibrations.

Wait several hours before completing this test again—whether about your child or about you.

To Identify the Dominant Sense:

1. Count the number of **V's, A's,** and **F's** for each person separately. The maximum for any of the three is 20.

2. Enter the totals here. V _____ A _____ F _____
3. Which has the highest total? _____

If the highest total is **V,** the person is dominant in the Visual sense. He or she most often uses sight to perceive the world and most often uses visual images in remembering and thinking.

If the highest total is **A,** the person is dominant in the Auditory sense. He or she depends most often on hearing to know what is happening. This person relies on the spoken word to obtain needed information.

If the greatest total is **F,** the person is dominant in Feelings. This person uses his/her feelings to sort what happens. The reactions to these feelings determine what he or she will do.

None of the three senses is superior to any of the others as a way of understanding and dealing with the world. Each of us is entitled to his/her own way of understanding and interacting with the world around us.

Translating Among The Senses

To enhance the perception of love, we need to improve the quality and clarity of communication between you and your children. The following examples and exercises will help you translate between the dominant senses. Remember, this is only a guide:

General: Please *consider* the possibility.
Visual: Please *examine* the possibility.
Auditory: Please *sound out* the possibility.
Feelings: Please *feel out* the possibility.

General: It *reminds* me of. . . .
Visual: It *looks* familiar.
Auditory: It *rings* a bell.
Feelings: It *strikes* me that. . . .

General: *attitude,*
Visual: *viewpoint,*
Auditory: *opinion,*
Feelings: *stance.*

General: *demonstrate,*
Visual: *show,*
Auditory: *explain,*
Feelings: *sort out.*

General: *Persevere.*
Visual: *See* it through.
Auditory: *Hear* it out.
Feelings: *Struggle* through it.

General: *absent,*
Visual: *blank,*
Hearing: *dumbfounded,*
Feelings: *empty.*

Now for some practice. Fill in the missing words.

General: *Identify.*
Visual: _____
Auditory: *Call attention to it.*
Feelings: *Put your finger on it.*

General: *plain,*
Visual: *lackluster,*
Auditory: _____,
Feelings: *dull.*

General: *ostentatious,*
Visual: *flashy,*
Auditory: _____,
Feelings: _____.

General: *exciting,*
Visual: *brighten the picture,*
Auditory: _____
Feelings: *tickles my fancy.*

General: *refer to,*
Visual: _____,
Auditory: *allude to,*
Feelings: _____.

The test and exercise are tools to help you understand differences between the communication styles used by your children and by you. But the best way to increase your skill and awareness at translating among the various sensory systems is to think about the language used by your children and yourself during conversation. You need lots of practice to do this effectively. In time, you will become attuned to the sensory language your children use, and you will automatically match it.

A hidden advantage of focusing on the dominant senses your children use is that you will become increasingly aware of communicating with the child. This requires that you listen to the words, hear how they are spoken, and attempt to understand the content. The process of improving communication is a big step toward improving your child's perception of being loved.

Don't try to change your child's dominant sense to match your own. Use your new knowledge to improve communication with the child—not to change the child.

CHAPTER 4

HOW DO YOU SHOW YOUR LOVE?

What are the twelve positive parenting styles?

In the last chapter we looked at how parenting and communication styles affect your children's perception of being loved. It is time now to take a closer look at twelve positive parenting styles—those styles that contribute most to the perception of love.

No two parents, or sets of parents, are identical. All parents bring their own beliefs, experiences, attitudes, and goals to the task of parenting. Some parents believe in a great deal of structure and control, while others are more comfortable with a free-flowing household. Some parents believe in safeguarding their children from possible mistakes, while others expect their children to learn from experience. Some parents believe in filling their children's days with planned activities, while others want their children to discover their own interests.

There is nothing "wrong" with any of these approaches. No one parenting style—within reason—is better or worse than any other, as we can see from the fact that children from widely divergent family systems can thrive and be happy. The key to parenting success depends less on your style of parenting than on creating a loving environment. Nevertheless, research shows that certain behaviors are more likely to foster a perception of love than others.

Through interviewing and surveying many youngsters, and studying research by other scientists, we have identified twelve positive parenting behaviors, or parenting styles, that seem to contribute most to children's perceptions of love:

- moderate freedom;
- positive evaluation;
- sharing;
- expressing affection;
- emotional support;
- intellectual stimulation;
- being child-centered;
- being possessive;
- being protective;
- encouraging sociability;
- encouraging independent thinking;
- treating your child as an equal.

Let's take a closer look at these twelve positive parenting styles.

What are the characteristics of the twelve positive parenting styles?

Moderate Freedom

Children function well in an environment where they have freedom of action within defined boundaries. They thrive by assuming responsibility for their own behavior and being allowed to make mistakes—all of this while accepting limitations based on real parental concerns. There are three areas in which parents may take action to increase the child's perception of some level of freedom about their own behavior:

- *Selecting and associating with friends.* Among toddlers and preschoolers, friendships are usually brief and task-oriented. Friends serve particular purposes, such as being a playmate for a game. Older children look for friends with whom they feel comfortable and are able to share feelings.

• *Budgeting and spending money.* It is difficult to feel independent when you have to ask for money—easily confirmed by any adult who is unemployed, on welfare, or tied to a spouse's checking account.

• *Making plans without having the prior consent of parents.* For young children, parents need to be actively involved in setting boundaries, rules, and curfews. As children mature and become capable of thoughtful decision-making, their actions no longer need to be micromanaged.

Positive Evaluation

Children gain self-esteem by reflecting how other people treat them. It is also known that parents are the most important people in a child's life. It follows, then, that the way in which children believe they are being treated by their parents will impact their self-image and behavior. The lack of positive evaluation will diminish a child's sense of self-worth, potential, and ultimately, behavior.

Positive evaluation is communicated to children when parents:

• *tell* the child the positive things they see about the child and what the child is doing;

• *do* things to convey nonverbally the positive things they see about the child and what the child is doing;

• *both tell and show* other people their pleasure with their child's behavior and personality.

Sharing

Sharing is a process of inclusion. It helps the child become part of his/her parents' lives and not just an expensive dependent. It is the *act* of sharing that is important to the showing of love, and not particularly *what* is being shared.

Early in life, children are urged to share things with their siblings—toys, food, sweets, and parental affection. Often it is done grudgingly, but sharing does take place. Sharing *things* doesn't usually involve a great deal of trust. Sharing thoughts and activities requires a far greater level of trust than sharing things. Things can be replaced; thoughts, activities, and feelings are more difficult to replace.

Parents may foster the *sharing* of *thoughts* by:

- talking things over with the children and progressively dealing with more complex and abstract issues;
- listening and reflecting while the child works through a difficult experience;
- listening and reflecting while the child works through and evaluates possible solutions to problems;
- sharing their own childhood growth experiences with the children;
- discussing parent problems and solutions with the children, being mindful of the children's ages and maturity.

Parents may foster the *sharing of activities* with their children by:

- working at having enjoyable and productive experiences at home;
- showing pleasure when on drives, trips, or visits with the children;
- taking the children to work with them;
- encouraging the children to make things and do things together with the parents.

Expressing Affection

Among very young children, unambiguous and visible affection from parents is expressed effectively by touching, hugging, holding, and rituals of physical care. If affection is expressed in subtle and abstract ways, only older, more emotionally mature children will understand. Thus, the way in which parents express affection must change to match the maturity level of the child.

However, being physically affectionate is acceptable in some cultures but frowned upon in others. For example, in some cultures kissing between males is widely accepted. In the United States, one must walk a fine line to avoid giving offense in deciding how and when to greet a member of the opposite sex with a kiss on the cheek or an embrace. Cultures differ in their norms for verbal demonstrativeness of affection, as well.

Family history and culture have much to do with the manner in which love and caring are shown. Generally speaking, parents may express affection both physically and verbally to children of all ages by:

- speaking to them in a warm and affectionate tone;
- smiling frequently at the children;
- telling children that they are missed when they are away from home;
- embracing younger children at night before they go to sleep;
- embracing children at any age, but in a nonsexual way;
- kissing the children on their cheeks when they arrive at home or when they leave;
- establishing special routines of care, shared activities or communication (an after-school task, a Saturday drive, family mealtimes, all examples of demonstrating affection.);
- establishing routines for safety and health (from seat belts to toothbrushing to bike helmets to fire drills) that signal a fundamental concern for the child's well-being and contribute to a sense of security in younger children.

Emotional Support

All humans need emotional support in the face of difficulties and unhappiness. Our children look to us for help, even though they may not be able or willing to ask for it. A thoughtful parent offers support in the following ways:

- Cheer the child when the child is sad. Accept the child's sadness as real, although it might appear trivial to the parent. Teasing humor without ridicule and sarcasm will help lighten the mood.

- Acknowledge that the child has a right to feel sad or angry but that the parent is there to help—when and if needed.
- Listen without comment or reaction. This can also provide considerable emotional support.
- Avoid judging the child. No one can offer support and sit in judgment at the same time. Wait until the crisis has passed before extracting any lessons from the situation to be learned and discussed.
- Encourage the child to persevere in seeking a solution to the problem. Younger people seek quick solutions, which might not be appropriate nor actually solve the problem. The parent can help the child plan and take that crucial first step.
- Praise the child for facing the problem. The word "encourage" literally means "to give courage."
- Hear the child's frustration, empathize with it, and gently try to convert it into a positive problem-solving force.

Intellectual Stimulation

To maintain good physical health, we are all advised to eat right and get plenty of exercise. Promoting good mental abilities also requires conscious effort. Today's family members are so involved in planned activities—both at work and play—that they have little time to indulge in intellectual fun. Parents can provide intellectual stimulation in the following ways:

- Depending on the age of the children, conduct a rhyming game or contest, have a spelling bee, or play ghost and other word games.
- Engage in a discussion with older children about current issues and major events of the day.
- Solicit children's opinions about a community event or problem, and then add to the children's information.

Being Child-Centered

During the first few years of life, a child is usually the center of the parents' universe. This attitude promotes a sense of security in the child, a wonderful feeling of being special and loved. As the child grows, matures, and strives for independence, the wise parent tries to balance the focus on the child with a broader view of family and the world around them. A completely child-focused parent fosters the development of a highly egocentric, narcissistic child.

The entrance into puberty and emerging adolescence exacerbates the situation. A normal phase of early adolescence is egocentricity and playing to an imaginary audience. Parents can help children mature into the real world as follows:

- Make children aware of the rest of the parents' universe, including work, hobbies, religious activities, and friendships.
- Help reframe the children's view of their own world to include other siblings and the parents' own needs.
- Ask the child to describe the needs of other members of the family when the child is attempting to satisfy only his or her own wants.

Being Possessive

Starting very early in life, every child needs to feel he/she is part of a family—meaning that the child both owns and is owned by the family. As children grow and mature, they still want to be connected to the family but no longer want to be completely owned by it. Overly possessive parents may destroy their child's self-esteem, initiative, and independence. The line between being overly possessive and providing a sense of belonging is often defined through trial and error. Generally speaking, here's how parents can demonstrate a healthy degree of possessiveness:

- Describe the qualities that the child has in common with both older family members (parents and grandparents) and siblings.
- Express interest in the child's activities along with reasonable concerns about health and safety issues—raising cautions without creating terror.
- Encourage the children to do things on their own and with their peers, increasing the level of independence based on experience and maturity.

• Do not intrude on children's privacy by reading personal journals, letters, or eavesdropping on telephone conversations.

Being Protective

A caring, involved parent will often spend much time and energy protecting the children from all manner of perceived problems—some real and some imagined. If the protection is total and continues for a very long time, the cocoon of love becomes a smothering experience. If combined with the problem of possessiveness described in the previous section, being overly protective will be very damaging to the long-term well-being of the child and to the perception of love.

As parents wrestle with the amount of protection to provide for their children, they need to balance the "downside risk" of not providing sufficient protection. When children are facing physical harm or danger, parents usually know what has to be done. To protect young children, parents secure kitchen-cabinet drawers, cover electrical outlets, and shield the oven or range. But it is far more difficult to decide whether to protect children from the lessons learned from failure or a mistake. Researchers have found that when children take personal blame for failure and credit their environment (others, including parents) for success, they grow and prosper. When they take personal credit for success and blame their environment (others, including parents) for their failure, their growth is slowed and stymied.

Parents can demonstrate an appropriate degree of protectiveness:

• Allow children to take "prudent risks" in forming new relationships. A certain amount of failure or mistakes is necessary to learn.

• Encourage children to discuss the possible dangers or problems of a proposed activity. During the discussion, parents can explain the various problems and offer suggestions about how to avoid trouble.

- Examine their own fears and needs before imposing them on their children.
- Be careful not to create false or unnecessary hurdles that become a tempting challenge for the children to overcome.

Encouraging Sociability

Children need well-developed social skills to interact with younger children, same-age peers, older children, and adults in a variety of settings throughout the day. Many of these settings—school and home, for example—are controlled by adults. In these adult-controlled settings, the adults spend much of their time instructing children about how they should behave. Parents routinely break up fights between siblings and espouse rules for sharing and fairness. But parents do all this from a position of authority—as both the judge and the jury. Children also need to learn how to interact with age and power equals—their peers.

Although most children interact daily with peers in a variety of unsupervised settings, parents still have a huge influence. Parents serve as role models on how to treat their own age peers and how one can expect to be treated by them. There are several areas in which parents can increase children's peer-related social skills:

- Since children learn how to deal with and interact with people of their own age by observing how their parents interact with other adults, parents need to avoid acting belligerently toward other adults in front of the children. Similarly, they need to be aware of any temptation to be accepting, complacent, or passive. Parents need to set a balance between independence, appropriate aggressiveness, assertiveness, and affability.
- Parents who disrespect their children, and who use ridicule and sarcasm as a style of interaction, encourage their children to treat others in that same way. Disrespect for the child encourages a reverse disrespect for adults and eventually, authority figures.

Encouraging Independent Thinking

Not all of the ideas generated by children are good. Conversely, not all of the ideas generated by children are impractical or harebrained. Parents need to work on improving the process of helping children generate new ideas and then sorting out those that are worth trying.

Parents can encourage their children to think independently by:

- not summarily rejecting the children's ideas;
- urging them to think in unorthodox ways to solve problems;
- brainstorming as a joint parent-child process;
- allowing children the opportunity to test their new idea;
- allowing children to select their own way to do things—at least some things.

Treating Your Child as an Equal

Parents who try to treat their children as their equals contribute greatly to improving the children's self-esteem. Being treated as an equal by parents makes children feel good about themselves. However, such treatment must have a basis in reality. For example, if your child knows much about playing a computer game and you also play computer games, it is realistic to treat your child as your equal in discussing the computer game.

While parents usually feel free to disagree with their child's viewpoint, it isn't often that children feel free to disagree with their parents. By agreeing to disagree, it is possible to create a positive, open environment for discussion where children feel a sense of equality. Here are some steps parents can take to increase their children's perception of being treated as an equal:

- Engage in appropriate and good-natured give-and-take, joking or teasing together.
- Encourage children to express and evaluate their opinions about things.

- Provide information to help children make decisions rather than making the decisions for them.
- Acknowledge the children's special skills and areas of growing expertise.
- Respect children's intelligence.
- Respect and value diversity in the family, including interests, tastes, and activities.
- Don't talk down to children.

By incorporating these twelve positive parenting styles into your interactions with your children, you will enhance and strengthen their perception of being loved.

CHAPTER 5

HOW DO CHILDREN PERCEIVE LOVE?

Do you know the "five W's" for perceiving love?

As we've said earlier, your children don't passively accept every-thing you say and do at face value. As their abstract-thinking abilities mature, they begin to judge and evaluate your behav-ior. It's an instinctive reaction, something they are probably not even aware they're doing. It's not that they're turning against you. It's an inevitable part of the process of growing up.

In practical terms, this means that they begin to experi-ence strong reactions to your styles of parenting and commu-nicating. They perceive unspoken (and spoken) messages about your feelings toward them. To complicate matters even further, their perception is colored by the "five W's"—the five criteria we all use to determine whether or not another's ac-tions toward us are loving. Those criteria that play such a big role in your children's perception of love are:

- **What** the parent does—actions.
- **Why** (in the child's opinion) the parent does it—motiva-tion.
- **When** the parent does it—timing.
- **Which** option the parent chooses—options.
- **Who** benefits by what was done—benefits.

Now let's examine how each of these criteria comes into play in your relationship with your children.

Actions

If you wish to convey love to another person—adult, adolescent, or child—you have to *do* something. It is impossible to convey love without taking some sort of action. Without some overt action on your part, the person to whom you wish to convey love would have to learn to read your mind and you would need the gift of telepathy. In fact, nowhere is the old adage "actions speak louder than words" more true than when expressing love.

We know a young man who was studying biomedical engineering at a prominent southern university. During the first half of his senior year, he was required to take a "killer course." Killer courses are required for graduation and are—naturally—notoriously difficult. Often, they are used as a final screening before graduation. And this young man was suffering. His self-esteem was going downhill as rapidly as his quiz grades for the course.

During a telephone call home, he told his parents that he was thinking of voluntarily dropping out rather than facing the disgrace of flunking out. Immediately his father and mother drove to the university for the weekend. Together they examined the situation. In the end they all agreed that giving up without a full effort to succeed wasn't very logical. The mother also pointed out that she had failed a course in college—the only one in her entire life—and she lived to tell the tale. By the time the parents departed, the son was reinvigorated and "went for it." He passed by the "skin of his teeth," but he passed.

He has since told his parents how important it was to him that they dropped everything to support him when he needed it. On their part, his parents expressed their love for him through their *actions*.

Not every act of love needs to be so memorable. In fact, it is in our small daily actions that we can express our love most meaningfully. When we offer praise and encouragement;

when we take the time to listen; when we drive a child to a friend's house or a favorite activity—in the innumerable acts that make up our daily routine, we have opportunities to express love through action.

When asked, most people describe the action of showing love as the primary force that allows a child to perceive love. While it is important, the other four factors are also essential. If actions alone were the only criteria, there would be far fewer problems with the perception of love by children.

Motivation

In criminal law and in justice, differences in a perpetrator's intent are reflected both in the charges and often in the punishment meted out. Crimes without malicious intent are often treated more leniently than those where the malice is evident. The difficulty is in correctly assessing the nature of the intent or motivation to commit the crime.

In the arena of love there is a similar difficulty. Children (like adults) often look behind actions to discover the *motivation*. Their perception of parents' motives will significantly color their perception of whether an action is an expression of love.

For example, consider a father who attempts to have a conversation with his adolescent son. Speaking in a warm and friendly voice, he asks about his son's friends: Who are they? What are their interests? Who are their families? Then "out of the blue" he suggests that his son invite his friends over for a party. What is his son to think? He might see his father's behavior as an act of love and caring. But if he detects another motivation—perhaps an attempt to manipulate and control his choice of friends—his father's actions will fail the test of being perceived as love.

Or think of a mother who uncharacteristically begins to talk with her daughter about the joys of watching her grow up. She compliments her daughter on her maturity and her skill at problem-solving. She makes a major point of complimenting her daughter's sense of responsibility. Then she says, "I know I can count on your help. I want to attend a special meeting at your school tomorrow night and I need you to 'sit' for your brother." Her daughter is left wondering whether her mother really meant the nice, affectionate things she said, or was she self-serving and setting her up to baby-sit for her brother?

Motivation also comes into question in the area of discipline. Appropriate structure and discipline are essential in child rearing. Parents express love when they take the time to teach right from wrong. But children will not perceive such action as love unless they understand the motivation.

If physical punishment, such as spanking or beating, is used, few children will accept that the pain and humiliation is for "their own good." Punishment must be used to teach without destroying children's self-image or perception of love from their parents.

A single mother had a particularly difficult evening with her twelve-year-old daughter. The daughter decided that she wanted her mother to buy something for her, and the mother said no. After a tension-loaded, uncomfortable dinner, the daughter started to whine. You've all heard that whine—it sounds like a train whistle racing down the track, alternating a loud blast with a quieter audible sigh. At first, she whined in her room. When the mother closed her door to the master bedroom, the daughter moved from her bed to right outside that door. After about fifteen minutes of hearing whining on her doorstep, the mother moved toward the door. The daughter heard the mother's approach and immediately retired to her bedroom. As the mother entered her room, the daughter was curled in a fetal position on the bed continuing the infernal whining. The mother sat next to her on the bed and asked, "Have you ever gotten what you wanted by doing what you are doing now?"

She stopped whining and gave her mother a puzzled look, which gradually changed into a knowing smile. Without a word, she closed her eyes and went to sleep. The mother had promised her nothing, nor had she threatened her. Her motivation was to teach that this behavior wouldn't work. She had thought of the right thing to say at the right time.

If the father in our first example had expressed interest in his son's friends and activities over time, then the current discussion and offer of a party would have been consistent with his past practices, creating a far better likelihood that his motivation would be seen as positive. Similarly, if the first mother had a consistent pattern of saying nice, affectionate things to her daughter *before* asking for a "favor," her daughter would not be suspicious of her mother's actions and would perceive them as showing love.

Inconsistent parent behavior confuses children. A consistent pattern of loving behavior increases the likelihood that actions and motivation will be perceived as love. However, these two factors are not sufficient in themselves to guarantee a perception of love.

Timing

It is possible for parents to do precisely the right thing for the best possible reasons but to do it at the worst possible time. Parents who want their children to perceive the love they feel can be clearly in control of the actions they take. Through introspection and self-awareness, parents can understand and, if necessary, change their motivation for taking the action. However, to find the *right time* to show love and have it perceived as love by the child requires several levels of awareness and understanding.

Receptivity in children varies as a result of their maturation: growing, developing, and changing. When parents want to show love, they need to try to be aware of the many things happening in their child's life, a task that *can seem* hopeless. They need to be aware of their child's friends and friendships, of "magical thinking" and being on "center stage" while the whole world is believed to be watching, and of narcissism and egocentricity.

Several years ago, a prominent psychologist who specializes in adolescence told us about her fourteen-year-old daughter. The psychologist noticed that her daughter recorded every item of clothing she wore each day in a special diary. The mother was astounded to see that *every* piece of clothing was noted. When asked why she kept such copious records about her clothing, the girl answered, "To make sure that I don't wear exactly the same clothing combination again—after all, someone might notice."

Now imagine the impact if this mother were to compliment her daughter on her appearance (a positive evaluation showing love) and suggest that she wear that outfit again soon. Her daughter might interpret the suggestion as a subversive act, or an example of sheer stupidity! Such an error might be avoided by recognizing the daughter's preoccupation with an "imaginary audience"—the belief that everyone is looking at her. While a rational parent might question whether anyone would want to be aware of every article of clothing worn by an adolescent, the adolescent dealing with the imaginary audience would not have any doubt. And that's what's important.

As children enter adolescence and puberty, their bodies and minds are in a constant state of change. Their moods swing through an enormous arc—from being elated, positive, and Pollyanna-ish to depression and self-loathing. Our difficulty as parents is to select the right moment to convey love so that the child might perceive that love. To see the level of difficulty, imagine a ball being bounced rapidly from six feet in the air and you, the parent, blindfolded and given only one chance to hit the ball on its way up or only one chance to hit the ball on its way down. Every now and then, you might get lucky and hit the target. Fortunately, we already know that the mood will shortly swing the other way and you'll have another chance at it.

Timing isn't everything—but a great deal may depend on getting it right once in a while.

Options

Three female college students sharing an apartment in Medford, Massachusetts, covered the refrigerator door with notes, small posters, and miscellaneous information. A pink knitted sweater that would fit a small doll was mounted on a piece of poster board. Above the sweater was the hand-written comment, "Aren't mothers wonderful?"

One well-intentioned mother had come to visit and decided to help with laundry and other household chores. In the process, she had laundered her daughter's favorite sweater without taking into account the necessary methods to avoid shrinkage. Her daughter told her friends, "I know my mom did it to be nice and she really loves me. But I wish she had found some other way to help."

Sound familiar? Your child appreciates what you did. Your child perceives that you care. And somehow, if you had just done something else, the child would have perceived a little more love. It works the same way for adults, too.

A harried mother with four adolescent sons was surprised when three of them announced that they had just washed and polished the family car. They had heard and understood her requests for help in trying to keep the family fed, housed, and clean. She responded, "I appreciate your washing and polishing the car. But I really need help in folding the four baskets of clothes sitting in the laundry room." In this example, we see how choosing the right *options* works both ways. The children wanted to express love, their mother perceived love, but she nevertheless wished that they had chosen to demonstrate their love by helping in a way that was important to her.

Among the four factors that we have discussed so far that determine whether a child perceives love—*actions, motivation, timing,* and *options*—the option the parent selects as a way of showing love probably contributes or detracts the least. If the parent has considered the other three factors, then selecting a better option won't add much to the perception of love. However, if the perception of love is borderline, a more carefully selected option might make a positive difference.

Benefits

The fifth and final factor used in deciding if a child perceives love is to estimate who *benefits* from what the parent has done. There are parents who *always* sacrifice for their children. By sacrificing frequently and letting the children know of the ongoing sacrifices, these parents enable the children to benefit—but at a price. Unfortunately, the sacrifices may be used to create guilt feelings in adolescents and serve to maintain tighter parental control for a longer period of time.

There are parents who *occasionally* sacrifice for their children. Some may sacrifice this way to enhance their own self-esteem. But we suspect that most do it out of love for their children, and do it willingly and in relative silence.

It helps immeasurably if we as parents know why we give up our desires, and whether we do it for our children's or our own benefit. It also helps to understand that the best actions are those from which both *children and their parents* gain some benefit.

Noted anthropologist Ruth Benedict, Margaret Mead's teacher and a strong cultural relativist, once confessed that even she was happiest visiting cultures organized so that what was good for one individual was good for the group, and vice versa. In such cultures, loving gestures and achievements were seen as spread or shared across a family network. The ideal is not to create a child-centered structure in which children are the primary beneficiaries of adult actions. Instead, actions are understood to be motivated by the desire to benefit the family unit, as well as its individual members.

Consider, for example, two families who live about 500 feet from each other. Both have adolescent sons who are approaching their seventeenth birthdays—two days apart—the legal age for obtaining a driver's license in their state. Both fathers are professionals owning and operating their own businesses. Although both men work very hard, they make sure that quality time is available to be devoted to their sons.

As their sons approach the days for taking the driver's license road test, both fathers arrange their schedules to accompany their sons—a licensed driver has to accompany the learner to the test site. Father #1 accompanies his son, who passes the test and drives home jubilantly. Father and son enjoy a celebratory lunch together. Father #2 has a last-minute problem and has to send one of his employees to accompany his son to the test. Son #2 also passes the test and drives home jubilantly. In conducting our test of perception of love, do both sons perceive love?

Yes. Although the fathers arrived at different solutions as the situation demanded, both sons perceive love. They both have histories of warm, affectionate, caring relationships with their high-achieving fathers. They both clearly benefit from their father's actions. And their fathers benefit, as well—father #1 by being present during his son's driving test; father #2 by being able to take care of pressing business matters.

This example illustrates our point that the most desirable actions are those from which both *children and their parents* gain some benefit.

As we have seen, children's perception of love is based on:

- *what* the parent does;
- *why* the child thinks the parent has done it;
- *when* the parent does it;
- *which* option the parent chose;
- *who* benefits by what was done.

What, why, when, which, and who benefits—if taken together, these five "W's" can unlock the mystery of how a child perceives love. The same combination can also unlock the mystery of how anyone perceives love and caring from another person.

CHAPTER 6

PUTTING IT ALL TOGETHER

How do parenting styles relate to "what, why, when, which, and who"?

So far, we have presented two important concepts: that children perceive love based on action, motivation, timing, options, and benefits (the what, why, when, which, and who of love), and that certain parenting styles contribute to the perception of love.

In the following illustrations we will see how these two concepts interact to create children's perception of parental affection. We have included some examples featuring children of different age groups, to show how the principles apply as children mature.

Moderate Freedom

Suzanne says that she trusts fourteen-year-old David's judgment most of the time, but David wants much more autonomy than his mother thinks he can handle. He believes that Suzanne tries to exert too much influence over his choice of friends. She also watches over the way his friendships develop. Recently Suzanne refused to drive him across town to a new friend's house because she felt that the new friend always lookcd sloppy and dirty.

David has been earning extra money by cutting lawns and

doing handiwork for neighbors. Suzanne insists that he bud-get the money "wisely" and discuss how he wants to spend it with her. David argues that he earned the money and should be allowed to spend it any way he wants. And he bristles at his mother's requirement that he ask her permission before he does anything. He was furious that Suzanne vetoed his plan to attend a rock concert, even though his friends and he would take public transportation and would return before his curfew of 11 P.M.

This ongoing interaction between Suzanne and David is being carefully watched by David's younger brother, Seth. At ten years of age, Seth idolizes his older brother and wants to be just like him. Seth trusts his mother and father. But some-thing is wrong. David is not happy. Suzanne is not happy.

ACTION

Sound judgment is a prerequisite for expanding David's opportunity to make his own choices, and it has to have been developed through experience. If Suzanne has been working at helping David evaluate situations and anticipate the conse-quences of his actions, she should recognize that he is ready to handle more decisions—although he can and will make mistakes. Perhaps she can begin by allowing David to dress like his peers, at least during his free time, or to have his hair cut in a style of his own choosing. She can stipulate that stylis-tic choices of a more irrevocable nature, such as body-piercing or tattooing, still require informed consent.

The operative word in granting freedom is "moderate." There is no need for Suzanne to give in to peer standards, the proverbial "everybody's doing it." She might work out a mutu-ally agreeable schedule with David to cover his time with friends, doing homework, athletics, and other activities. The parental role is to guide and inform, not to mandate or order. Suzanne might back off from tight control by allowing David to stay awake later without asking permission, or by allowing him to negotiate his own curfew.

Teaching David effective control of his earnings requires great delicacy. While it is true that he earned the money, his mother still needs to teach him fiscal responsibility. David should be allowed to develop his own budget in which he spends some money on indulgences and leisure, gives some to charity, and saves the rest. As a start, he might begin to pay for some of his personal needs—for instance, articles of clothing he's now allowed to wear.

There is not much difference in how Suzanne grants moderate freedom to David as compared to Seth. Seth is at an earlier stage of assuming autonomy. For example, Suzanne might allow Seth to set his own curfew one night each week. Also, Seth's weekly allowance from his parents provides a good learning experience for the family in helping Seth budget his income.

MOTIVATION

There is no guarantee that over the shorter term, the child will perceive a parent's motivation for wanting to grant moderate freedom. It is more important for the parent to understand his/her own reasons. These reasons might include the following five desires:

- showing that you trust your child;
- showing an awareness that your child is growing up;
- helping your child become an independently functioning adult;
- teaching the child to tolerate errors as part of the learning process;
- recognizing the child's maturing judgment and abilities.

TIMING

Granting freedom needs to be done in small increments. If you probe deeply enough, you will find that granting complete and total freedom to a child is not only unwise but also very frightening to the child. Most children desire structure and control in their lives along with moderate levels of freedom. If you, as the parent, carefully observe your children and attempt to understand their changing needs, you will most probably match the freedom you award with their needs and your household, family, and neighborhood circumstances. If you wait too long, the children will press you. If you grant the freedom too early, everyone will learn from the child's mistakes. But if the child is to grow, he/she will eventually need to make more decisions independently.

OPTIONS

There are many ways to show that you are learning to trust your children and are willing to grant them moderate autonomy. In addition to curfew and spending-money options, Suzanne might extend David's range of freedom in changing his daily or weekly schedule, visiting friends at home, and perhaps "staying over." Suzanne needs also to become more aware that David is at an age where the opposite sex will become increasingly appealing to him. She needs to consider how to grant David sufficient freedom to explore the emerging social world of interacting with girls. Remembering what it was like to be David's age might be helpful, although it would likely be tempting to remove the pain of mistakes *she* made at that age.

BENEFITS

As children gain experience in using their freedom, their decision-making will improve and they will gain confidence. As you grant freedom and it is used more wisely than before, you will become more comfortable with granting additional freedom and you will gain by having a less dependent child. Both parent and child gain from the effective granting of moderate freedom.

Positive Evaluation

Charles Horton grew up in a family where open displays of affection were frowned upon. Compliments to family members were viewed as being boastful and improper. Expressing delight in the accomplishments of a family member was discouraged. As Charles grew up, his inability to display affection prevented him from providing positive, reinforcing feedback to other people. When his daughter, Michelle, was born,

Charles continued to behave the same way. He could not bring himself to compliment Michelle or to tell other people positive things about her. His style was also to "bring Michelle down a peg" when she appeared to become "too full of herself."

Now at age ten, Michelle is aware that her father smiles at her and seems happy to see her when he comes home from work. But that's where it seems to end.

Michelle feels increasingly hurt by her father. The hurt is rapidly becoming a perception that her father doesn't love her. She believes he's disappointed in her but can't understand why.

ACTION

Charles is aware that he provides little positive feedback to Michelle. He has sensed that his relationship with her is deteriorating. While much of Charles' behavior is determined by his family culture, he can still make a positive change. Charles loves Michelle, but he needs to find ways for her to know that he loves her.

As a start, Charles should try to identify positive things about Michelle that he feels capable of conveying to her. He knows that she has perseverance and athletic skills, is creative and is liked by most people. He could practice telling her that he is proud of something specific she has done or said. When he comes home from work, instead of just smiling at her, he might inquire about her day's activities and express some pleasure at something that she has done.

He needs to "start small." He could tell Michelle's mother, grandparents, aunts, uncles, cousins, and close friends positive things about Michelle. He must continue to express pleasure at seeing and being with Michelle. Charles might have to "fake it" at first, until he can become acclimated to providing the positive evaluation Michelle and he both need.

MOTIVATION

Unless Charles changes his behavior, Michelle's self-esteem will suffer. She is already puzzled by his perceived distance and lack of positive evaluation. If reinforced over time, she will come to see it as her failure; perhaps she is not worthy of being loved. Thus, a primary reason for providing positive evaluation for Michelle is to develop and maintain a positive self-concept. Charles is also aware that he's missing something—loving and being loved by his daughter.

TIMING

Charles should praise Michelle *immediately after* she does something praiseworthy. Saving up the praise to be delivered once a week on a given day will not enhance her perception of being loved. The attempt at positive evaluation cannot be accomplished in fits and starts. Much praise today and little praise for the rest of the week is not likely to improve the situation.

At first, Charles should make a concerted effort to find praiseworthy events and activities—at a level where he is slightly uncomfortable. The effort at praise should continue until he becomes comfortable at that level and then proceed to the next level where again he is slightly uncomfortable. The method of praise should vary—the words used and the people spoken to should change. And then, Charles should again raise the effort to his next level of "discomfort."

OPTIONS

Since Michelle already knows that there is something askew in the way her father deals with her, perhaps there is another way to approach changing the situation. Charles can begin to describe his childhood and growing up in his family. As part of the description, he can detail his family's attitude toward praise and showing affection. He can tell Michelle that he wants to change but is finding it difficult. He might ask, "Can you help me?" Together they might develop their own language for praise and affection, which would meet her needs for hearing and feeling it and his need for being obtuse in his display.

BENEFITS

For Charles, it is very difficult to see Michelle—the child he loves—become distanced from him. In many ways, he feels incapable of being able to show how positive he feels about her. At a minimum, displaying positive evaluation of Michelle will increase Charles's happiness and sense of well-being. For Michelle, enhanced self-concept and a sense of well-being should also result. Both father and daughter will benefit.

Sharing

Christine Washington is excited about going to a neighborhood party where there will be some kids she knows from her high school, as well as kids from a high school in another part of the city. Susan, the girl who invited Christine to the party, is actually more of an acquaintance than a friend. During the party, Christine sees Susan smoking marijuana with a group of kids mostly from the other high school.

The next day, with Josh, Christine's seven-year-old brother standing nearby, the mother asks Christine about the party and whether she had a good time. Christine tells her mother about Susan smoking marijuana. Her mother is shocked and asks, "Did you smoke marijuana, too?"

"Of course not."

"Does Susan's mother know about this?"

"I don't think so."

Before Christine realizes what is about to happen, her mother dials Susan's telephone number. Susan's mother answers on the first ring. Christine's mother quickly describes the marijuana incident at the party. Susan's mother doesn't believe the story, becomes angry, and says that she will check with Susan.

Christine is in a state of shock. She confided in her mother, and her mother broke that trust. "How could you? I will never be able to face my friends again. I shared the information with you, and you betrayed me."

Josh is confused. He has been told many times that using drugs is wrong and will not be tolerated. He is sure that

Christine also knows that it is wrong. Josh is not yet old enough to comprehend the sense of betrayal felt by Christine. On the surface, the situation is clear. Christine saw her friend doing something "wrong" and told her mother. Why, then, is Christine so hurt and angry?

ACTION

In order to be able to share, you need to have some trust in the other person, because sharing involves taking a risk. In this situation, Christine shared her thoughts about the experience at the party because she trusted her mother. She trusted that her mother wouldn't do anything to embarrass her or to harm her peer relationships. If she had known that her mother would immediately call Susan's mother, she would not have said anything.

While her spontaneous reaction is understandable, Christine's mother did not respond well to the sharing of the information. The mother has devoted much time and effort to talking things over with Christine. At times, she has shared many of her own experiences—happy times and frustrations—from when she was growing up. More recently, she has begun talking about some family problems and possible solutions with Christine within earshot of Josh.

But the mother reacted too quickly and angrily to the marijuana incident. Among the reasons for the reaction was that she wanted Christine to know how strongly she was against the use of drugs. But Christine didn't have a chance to learn about any of the reasons—it all happened so quickly. The mother might have expressed her displeasure to Christine and listened to her daughter's thoughts. Together they might have searched for solutions about appropriate ways to behave. This might have led to an important discussion of values, standards, and feelings. Additionally, Christine would have had the opportunity to ask her mother not to make the telephone call to Susan's mother.

MOTIVATION

Parents have gone through experiences and have developed problem-solving processes and wisdom that they wish to give to their children. Children are not always receptive. With their striving for independence, children sometimes resent "being given to." One way around this struggle is to let the parental wisdom emerge in response to the child's requests, and through the sharing of things, thoughts, and activities. This aids in developing a genuine closeness with the children and helps build a higher level of trust and understanding between you and them.

Parents demonstrate ways of communicating, analyzing, and solving problems through sharing. They also model respect for the child's developing skills and personal qualities through listening while the child shares.

TIMING

A spontaneous offer to share things or activities, when your child hasn't asked, can be a very positive trust and relationship builder. However, if the offer is completely out of character for you, it could have the reverse impact—raising suspicion. Start with responding positively to requests for sharing—when possible. Later on, try a spontaneous offer.

Sharing with your children anecdotes about growing up is a wonderful way to establish rapport with them and to indicate how much you value your children and their qualities. For the young child, stories of adventure with humor will be enjoyed and remembered. Stories of challenge will signal they, too, can overcome obstacles. Stories of pathos and unpleasant experiences have to be fitted to the child's maturity and perceived ability to comprehend and accept such stories. Proceed slowly and share selectively.

OPTIONS

Christine's mother's intentions were good. Her reactions were instinctive. But she has some work ahead of her to restore Christine's trust. One option is to apologize to Christine for the hasty response—not for her opposition to smoking marijuana. Another would be to describe a situation in which she herself confronted a moral dilemma. The sharing may bring mother and daughter closer together.

Josh cannot be overlooked in the situation. He is learning by observing. He is also learning by being involved in the sharing of the achieved solutions.

BENEFITS

Sharing is built on trust. When parents create an environment in which children feel safe to share their feelings, children may be able to open up about serious issues they are likely to confront as they mature, including drugs and sexuality. The closeness that results from honestly sharing concerns and feelings strengthens the family unit, enriching all of its members.

Expressing Affection

Jesse is ten years old and in fifth grade. He appears to be well-adjusted. Academically he does well. In athletics, he has some talent for track and gets along well with his peers.

Marva, Jesse's mother, is a warm, affectionate person. She bathes Jesse in affection by kissing him when he leaves for school in the morning, hugging him when he comes home, and frequently telling him that she loves him. His father shows affection in other ways—frequently smiling at Jesse, enjoying doing things with Jesse, and speaking to him in a warm, affectionate tone.

One afternoon, Marva is driving past the school when school is letting out. She notices Jesse talking with his friends nearby. Marva stops the car near the curb and hurries to meet Jesse. She rushes up to him and says, "I was driving past and saw you. Would you and your friends like a ride home? Yes? We'll go as soon as I give you a big hug and a kiss." She moves to put her arms around him.

Jesse is mortified. He knows that his friends will tease him unmercifully and wonders why his mother did such a foolish thing.

ACTION

Marva may be doing too much of what could be a good thing. How much affection she is showing to Jesse is not the issue in this episode. The issue is what does Jesse perceive as affection. A parent might do many things to show affection—hugs, kisses, smiles, and delight in being with the child. In many families, these are all valuable, desired deeds. The child may desire that some exhibitions be done in private—and not in public. In particular, preadolescent and adolescent boys may have to learn to communicate about their comfort level with parental displays of affection in different settings and at different times.

Jesse may see his mother's action as an embarrassment and even as a put-down. The projected affection missed its mark. Marva could have offered the ride home to Jesse and his friends and then embraced Jesse when they were alone. Also, affection would still have been conveyed by the offer of a ride home and speaking to Jesse with warmth and affection. Simply put, Marva and Jesse had not worked out what Jesse sees as affection.

MOTIVATION

It feels good to express affection toward another person. Observe how adults behave with a baby: They play, smile, touch, coo, laugh, cuddle, and kiss. While they want to make the baby happy, the experience is good for them. Similarly, there is evidence that providing people with a companion animal that they can pet and love improves their physical and mental health. Of course, petting obviously soothes and changes the nervous system of the companion animal, as well, as any cat owner knows. The theme of this book is that the perception of being loved is "good" for children, but another reason for parents to express affection to their children is that it benefits them, too.

TIMING

There is one overriding aspect to the best timing for displays of affection: what works for both parties, parent and child. Affection must be comfortable for both. Some infants are squirmers; some are cuddlers. For some, touch gets them going; for others, touch calms them. Parents and kids negotiate what is perceived as affectionate and when to express affection from the beginning of life.

Generally, though, younger children understand the overt, concrete actions of physical affection. They are not yet ready to comprehend the abstractions inherent in subtle displays of affection and love. As children grow older, parents need to adjust their methods of expressing affection from overt to more subtle actions.

Another timing issue relates to the venue in which the display of affection occurs. Purely within the family setting, at home or alone with the child, the parent can be as overt in showing affection as the child likes. If the child is clearly uncomfortable, the parent can "back off" easily in a private setting. A public display of affection, where the parent cannot gauge the group and child's reaction in advance, leaves little room for error.

OPTIONS

Had Marva thought about it, she might have just driven on home and allowed her son and his friends to either walk or ride the school bus. It would have been only a few more minutes before she would have seen her son in the privacy of their home. Again, if Marva had thought about it, she might have offered a ride home for the group of boys without the quid pro quo from her son of a "big hug." The other options available to Marva would stem from her thinking about her son's feelings, not only her own.

BENEFITS

As described earlier in this section, a reason for parents to express affection to their children is that it is good for the parents. The theme of this book is that the child's perception of being loved portends good things for the child. Jesse has shown all the positive signs of being loved by his parents and perceiving it. Marva, too, has been enriched by showing love. Unfortunately, she has made a mistake. It is not fatal. As we have talked about earlier, Marva has "banked" a considerable amount of showing love and having it perceived. She just made a withdrawal.

Emotional Support

Eleven-year-old Letitia dreams of becoming a "modern dancer" and performing on Broadway. She has been taking lessons and studying for about three years. Clearly, Letitia has some talent, but whether she has the drive and ability to eventually dance as a professional is unclear. Recently the dance studio sponsored tryouts to win solo-dance opportunities at the school's annual recital. Letitia had her heart set on winning a solo-dance position. Unfortunately, she places out of the running.

For a week after the tryouts, Letitia was inconsolable. She was sad, difficult to be with, and struggling to salvage her self-esteem. Her mother, Joanne, listened to Letitia's lament and said, "I know you feel bad but it is better to discover now that you don't have enough talent to make it in the big time." She also went on to say, "In time, you'll be better off giving up dancing and learning something more practical for your future." Letitia became sadder and more unhappy.

ACTION

Instead of demolishing Letitia's hopes by telling her that she has limited talent and should be thankful she learned it early in life, her mother could help her think through the reasons for the intensity of her disappointment. Once the reasons are identified, Letitia can be guided on two levels: one, managing her emotions; two, putting the experience in perspective. Joanne can help her daughter take a more realistic view of failing one audition and go on to discuss other needed training or career choices.

Joanne should encourage exploration rather than render a harsh, immediate judgment. In fact, other dance professionals, rather than the mother, may be the best source of advice.

MOTIVATION

There are times when each of us has had a shock to our hopes and dreams. After such a shock, we become more vulnerable to negative changes in our lives. It can be shown that people are far more susceptible to persuasion during periods of major change or crisis in their lives. Joanne needs to provide emotional support for Letitia to allow her to learn from the experience and to alter her plans for the future. Without such support, Letitia might persuade herself that she has little or no worth to anyone, and that the future holds little promise.

TIMING

Time can heal many wounds. Letitia may learn over the next few years that she has limited ability to compete with other trained dancers. She may well discover other talents and skills, so the catastrophe of not landing the dancing lead will become minimal.

The problem for the parent is how to ease the wound without being dishonest with the child. Perhaps the most meaningful effort at the time of the problem would be merely to listen and assist in clarifying the situation.

OPTIONS

A modern dancer with three years of training has limited ability to compete with individuals with more training. One failed audition is not the end of a career. Eventually Letitia may decide to find another place for dance in her life. Or she might decide to expand her training. In time, Joanne might make the effort to suggest alternate careers. Knowing the child and having a positive, trusting relationship can help resolve the problem.

BENEFITS

Support when needed may often be classified as "uncondi-
tional love." Our children might not dance like Bob Fosse or
Cyd Charisse, but we love them just the same. They need to
know that our love for them has little to do with their successes or failures and that we love them for who they are. They
need also to learn that our "failures" are part of us—often an
enriching part. They make us humane and understanding of
others. They help us revise our plans or increase our will and
drive. They teach us how to treat others who are disappointed.
Giving emotional support helps children through difficult
times and strengthens our skills not only as parents but as caring human beings.

Intellectual Stimulation

It's report-card time again at the Lincoln Middle School.
When James's report card arrived at home, his father, Frank,
read it carefully, including a comment made by his home-
room teacher that "James is not achieving up to his potential."
The teacher believes that James is not being challenged intellectually—whether in school or at home.

Frank feels pangs of guilt. Both Frank and his wife are em-
ployed full-time, and then some. Although the parents have
hired a person to help provide child care, they are aware that
their jobs have allowed little time to be "involved, caring parents." Frank proposes that he reduce his time at work to
spend more time with his son. He obtains a reduction in time
at work and starts coming home at 3:30 in the afternoon.

With the help of his wife, Frank launches a plan to stimulate James intellectually. He greets James daily with questions
about school activities. He has implemented a plan where
James contracts with him to do a specific amount of weekly
reading. A computer is purchased and "thinking" software is
installed. At the end of the first two weeks, James rebels.
"What's going on? Have I done anything wrong? Okay, so I'm
coasting. I'll buckle down before too long. Slow down, Dad."
Frank is shocked. After all, he has made significant changes in
his life to devote time and energy to James.

ACTION

James has taken advantage of his parents' hectic schedule to coast and to operate well below his intellectual capacity. In attempting to overcome the problem, Frank has gone overboard—too much and too soon. Frank has to take into account the history of the situation, his son's intelligence, different alternatives, and finally, the shared goals of the entire family.

The school classroom is a formal learning environment. Subjects are taught according to a prepared academic curriculum. Both preteens and teens need to learn much more about life from parents, beyond what is taught in school.

Parents can talk about current events with their children to supplement classroom discussions. They can ensure that a quality newspaper or news magazine is available in the home. Parents might help children discover where needed information is available—including a visit to the library or an exploration of the Internet. A computer is an excellent addition to the repertoire for stimulating the child intellectually.

Generally, parents should not assume that their children will always tell them of significant events at school. Parents must ask meaningful questions and not just inquire, "Tell me what you did in school today." Any plan developed by Frank and his wife to stimulate James should have specific objectives, as well as both immediate and long-term activities. The effort must be sustainable over time, or else James will learn how to work and then coast until the storm blows over.

MOTIVATION

The conventional wisdom has been that increasing a child's self-esteem will lead to an improvement in academic achievement and achievement in other areas of life. Evidence from research suggests that the reverse is true—increasing achievement will enhance self-esteem. Thus, self-esteem is a desired result rather than only a means to improve academic achievement.

Additionally, obtaining a better job and earning a higher income are related to achievement, particularly academic achievement. Going to college, learning a skill or trade, and persevering beyond the norm require some level of intellectual and, often, academic achievement. Parents can help their children achieve these goals by providing intellectual stimulation.

TIMING

The timing for intellectual stimulation is heavily dependent on what is going on in the child's life. If the child is an athlete or loves to watch sports events, you can build upon sports to teach how to find information. Reading can be enhanced through athletes' biographies. Possible player trades and draft picks can be used to teach planning and development of strategies. Similarly, parents can build upon interests in nature, chemistry, astronomy, psychology, and other hobbies to enhance reading and other intellectual pursuits.

OPTIONS

By focusing on intellectual stimulation, Frank and his wife are increasing their demands on their son. They are raising their expectations of his performance and showing him that they are. Another option is to tell him that they believe he has greater capacity than he is using and that their job is to get him to use it. If done consistently and without anger, this might also have a positive impact on their son's self-esteem and performance.

BENEFITS

It has been often said that human beings use a very small part of their brainpower—some estimates say as little as fifteen percent. Providing intellectual stimulation to James may help him utilize more of his brainpower and more fully develop the part he is using. This will result in improved academic achievement and will bring about, in turn, enhanced self-esteem in James. A special additional benefit is the opportunity to have a shared activity in the family—one of the elements that enhances the perception of love.

Being Child-Centered

Paula is a thirteen-year-old only child attending a private middle school. Her parents, John and Kay, have detected major changes lately in the way Paula is thinking and behaving. She keeps a diary containing a description of each and every piece of clothing she wears each day. In addition, she acts as if the whole world is watching every move she makes. In fact, she behaves as if she is on a stage with an array of spotlights shining on her.

John and Kay have always made her the center of their lives. The things they do as a family are primarily the things Paula wants to do. They have given up many of the things they wanted in deference to what Paula wanted. They are centered on obtaining the best of everything for her. The parental focus has been on making Paula happy *as an individual* rather than being a happy family. Recently Paula has become an egocentric, difficult, and aloof individual. John and Kay are worried they've created a monster—one who takes but does not know how to give in return.

ACTION

John and Kay have provided *too much* of what once was a good thing. Overindulging Paula as a young child may have made them feel good as parents and brought considerable closeness to the family. Although there are no overt signs of it, John and Kay may inadvertently move toward future control of Paula's behavior by using "guilt." It is time for the parents to move toward a more equitable arrangement of meeting Paula's and their needs. Before dealing with Paula, they need to establish priorities about what is important to them. Where on their hierarchy of needs is Paula's schooling? Her entertainment? Her clothing? Their entertainment? Their hobbies?

The parents also need to understand more about the social, emotional, intellectual, and physical growth and development of their emerging adolescent daughter. This knowledge will help them in setting short- and longer-term priorities. Simply put, John and Kay need to balance being child-centered with being family-centered and with outreach to the larger society.

MOTIVATION

We suspect that many of the reasons for parents to become overwhelmingly child-centered derive from expectations they believe others have of them. The grandparents, extended family members, adult peers in the same socioeconomic group, and their social network, might have conveyed an impression that a successful family is one in which the complete focus is on the child. It is also possible that the complete focus on the child is a reaction to either one or both parents' feeling of neglect during childhood. Or, finally, the parents may have learned, by example, a strategy of control based on making the child feel guilty about all the things her parents have done for her.

There is a need in most families for some level of being child-centered—the children are usually the most needy members of the family for attention and support. The issue here is of degree.

TIMING

A dominant issue in modifying high levels of child-centeredness is the developmental stage of the child. In adolescence, children vacillate between egocentrism and a heightened sense of concern for others. It will take special patience and awareness by John and Kay to gradually change their focus of being Paula-centered to being family- and social-centered. It also requires understanding the developmental stages of early, middle, and late adolescence. Time and maturation will surely help Paula change but unless the change is guided, the egocentricity may only change its form and not its intensity.

OPTIONS

It is hard to live with extreme egocentrism and narcissism. This can be particularly difficult when John and Kay realize that they are greatly responsibile for it in Paula. The parents can reduce their focus on Paula to a much lesser degree, and then to do nothing. Doing nothing to maintain or increase the focus on Paula as she develops through adolescence, is likely to bring about changes in her. It is not likely that Paula's peers will tolerate extreme narcissism for long. Her parents' role will be to help her understand the peer reactions and to offer alternate behaviors.

BENEFITS

A moderately child-centered home environment bodes well for parents and children. Parents can create a family structure and environment that maintains some level of being child-centered while meeting the needs of other family members, including the parents. Likewise, they can strive to turn the family outward toward civic- and community-mindedness. John and Kay have gone beyond the needed level. Unlike Paula at this time, children who mature in a balanced environment learn a model of behavior that will serve them well when they seek to build interpersonal and social relationships.

Being Possessive

Susan is thirteen years old and very active in all types of athletic activities. Her recreation center's ski club has planned a one-day ski trip, including ski instruction for beginners. Susan has saved money for the trip. On the morning of the outing, Susan is ready to go, and her parents are waiting for her ride to pick her up.

Her mother warns, "Now be careful, Susan. Since you've made up your mind to go skiing, I want you to be careful."

Susan replies, "Mom, I'll be all right. I can take care of myself."

Her father says, "Honey, please call us collect as soon as you arrive at the slopes. I'm worried that the roads could be dangerous this time of the year."

Her mother adds, "I'm not sure this is a good idea. I never did dangerous sports when I was your age. Can you imagine what'll happen to your grades if you break your leg? If anything happens to you, I'd have to give up my job to stay home and take care of you."

Her father says, "She'll be careful. Won't you? Remember, if anything happens, call us first. We have a lot invested in you."

Susan protests, "Nothing will happen."

Her mother concludes, "Well, enjoy yourself. We'll want to hear all about the trip—everything—when you get back. Promise?"

ACTION

As in the other examples, Susan's parents have gone too far. First, it is not likely that when Susan returns, she will tell her mother "all about the trip—everything." At best, this is intrusive. At worst, it is a ridiculous request, and Susan will clearly ignore it. Asking Susan to call them first in the event of an emergency doesn't make much sense, either. In an emergency, Susan needs to contact whoever can help her at that time. A call to her parents would come later. Susan's parents don't seem to know how to let go and give her some independence. Her struggle to achieve independence has already started and will intensify.

When a child does well, parents feel pride in the accomplishment. In part, this can occur because the parents see the child as an extension of themselves. Or, it can be because the child is appreciated as a separate, surprising, and valuable individual. A glance at the cheering section at Little League games, school sports, music recitals, spelling bees, and other activities, will find parents fully involved and supportive. This support is needed whether the child does well or not. Participation and performance are risks for children. Success at an activity should not be a requirement for feeling part of a family or for perceiving love from parents. Nor should avoidance of failure or avoidance of normal bumps and bruises that accompany learning skills be the litmus test.

MOTIVATION

Some sense of possessiveness is necessary. Perhaps it is better described as providing a sense of belonging. Some children who lack a sense of belonging to a family seek it elsewhere. One place to seek belonging is in gangs. A gang structure provides this missing sense of belonging, often to a pathological level.

But possessiveness in Susan's situation has been taken to an extreme and is smothering. Primarily, the reason her parents have become overly possessive is fear—fear of Susan growing up, becoming independent, and physically and emotionally moving away. Parents who smother need to re-examine their fears about, and for, their children. By being overly possessive, they deprive the child of the experiences necessary to learn and grow.

TIMING

During unhappy periods, children have a greater need to return to the family bosom and be part of it. During times of independence and happiness, children are comforted to know that the parents care about them and can be drawn upon when needed. The parents need to be sensitive to events and conditions in their child's life to know when to vary their possessiveness. On occasion, too much possessiveness at the wrong time will result in being pushed away. But generally speaking, the parent-child relationship can tolerate an occasional mistake.

OPTIONS

Susan's parents could have withheld permission to go on the trip. This would have accomplished an unacknowledged goal of keeping her at home, under their control and safe from harm. The impact on their relationship with Susan and her perception of love would have suffered a severe blow, though. If they have raised a daughter with common sense, few of their admonitions about being careful and safe would have been necessary. If they raised a careless daughter, perhaps she shouldn't go on the trip. The point is, the preparatory work has been done already—she is an adolescent. They have given permission for the trip. Now is the time to hide their fears and wish her well.

BENEFITS

Most people have a need to be included in a close group—family, team, social club, company, organization, or gang. Somehow that sense of belonging provides comfort and a safety net in what is often perceived as a hostile world. The benefits of belonging are balanced against the deficits of being overwhelmingly possessed by the other group members, including family. The balance will change for both the parent and the child as part of the life cycle, and so will the benefits to both.

Being Protective

Mary Sullivan is tending her two preschool children at a playground adjoining the middle school. Suddenly, a racing bicycle comes hurtling through the playground, narrowly missing the children. A boy of about fourteen is still on his bike and is laughing. Mary screams at him in frustration and fear. He again laughs and says, "Cool down, lady. No one got hurt, did they?"

Mary recognizes the bicycle and the rider. She reaches into her purse and brings out her cell phone. She quickly obtains the telephone number of the bike rider's home and places a call. Without embellishing the story, she tells the rider's mother about what happened. The rider's mother says, "Since he didn't hurt anyone, what is there to complain about? We've been trying to make him more responsible and careful when riding his bike. Filing a complaint with the school or even the police will get him into trouble and won't help at all. Please understand."

Mary thinks about the situation for a short while and then calls the middle school and files the complaint.

ACTION

Not everyone will agree with Mary's action in calling the bike rider's mother. Others will agree that her action was appropriate to prevent the bike rider from endangering others. She was acting protectively for her children. However, so was the bike rider's mother. She was providing protection against trouble for her son and placing herself between the outside world and him. This can become an all-consuming effort. The alternative is to establish boundaries for behavior and allow the children to operate independently within those boundaries. If the boundaries are violated, then the child has to learn the consequences of his/her own behavior. And the bike rider appeared to be unaware of his boundaries. If the parent always intervenes, how can the child learn? Obviously, when life-threatening situations are possible, the boundaries would be drawn very tightly. But most situations for children are not life-threatening.

MOTIVATION

The bike rider's mother may have a sense of guilt that she is responsible for all actions by her son. Thus, by protecting children from the consequences of their actions, the parents assuage their own guilt. To some degree, this is probably correct. Parents guide the way children learn how to behave—at the least, they create the general guidelines. Children have to refine the learning through experience. And to gain the experience, they have to experiment. Mary's actions have a dual protective role—first, to protect her children from excessive danger; second, to ensure that the dangerous bike rider is not allowed to continue that behavior to endanger others.

TIMING

Being protective all the time relieves the child of the responsibility for learning how to behave. Parents should study and learn when protectiveness is appropriate for their children. In this anecdote, being protective of the bike rider is not the right move. The boy's parent could use this episode to draw narrower boundaries for endangering other people—

and must draw those boundaries immediately after the event and/or the complaint.

OPTIONS

The bike rider's mother is excusing her son's reckless behavior. She acknowledges a problem by saying she and her husband have been trying to make him more responsible. Obviously, they haven't succeeded. Mary might have used the threat of filing a complaint to force the parents to take more immediate action. This is clearly not her role nor her responsibility. She could have ignored the incident. While her children might not be the potential targets of reckless bike riding in the future, it is likely that other children will be. Mary considers her responsibility to the community an important part of her life.

BENEFITS

In an environment with the right balance of protection and independence, a child will learn how to cope with danger. However, there are some people who like to "live on the edge." They enjoy danger and taking risks. There are others who live safely and avoid taking undue physical risk. The protective envelope provided by parents has to expand and contract to foster the safety, as well as the growth, of the children while minimizing any sense of guilt or undue loss by parents.

Encouraging Sociability

Cindy Black is a single mother of a twelve-year-old girl named Judith. Last summer, Cindy and her daughter moved from a large city into an apartment in a pleasant, smaller neighborhood. Judith enrolled in school, and when school began in the fall, she tried to make new friends. She was having a difficult time entering the friendship cliques and was becoming increasingly unhappy.

Cindy was also trying to get involved in the community and trying to make friends. She volunteered to help the tenants association and became the chairperson of a three-person subcommittee developing the holiday-decorations policy of the apartment complex. One night Cindy conducted a meeting in her apartment while Judith watched TV in an adjoining room. Judith overheard her mother repeatedly saying such things as "I'm new to the neighborhood. I'm sure you know what the policy should be," or "Whatever you say is all right with me." Cindy was clearly going out of her way to agree with everything her neighbors suggested.

As winter approached, Judith became more unhappy. She was feeling disliked and unwanted. Cindy learned that Judith's social studies teacher had divided the class into small study groups for a special assignment. She suggested that Judith invite the other two girls on her team to come to their apartment after school, spend the afternoon working on the assignment, and then all have dinner together. The girls accepted the invitation.

As Cindy was preparing dinner, she heard the discussion among the three girls. Judith made no attempt to influence the direction of the team. She passively accepted any and all recommendations from the other two students. She curried favor by praising any suggestion or comments they made. Cindy could not contain herself and entered the room saying, "Judith, you and I have discussed some of your excellent ideas about this. How about sharing them with your team?"

ACTION

Cindy started out well. She encouraged Judith to bring friends home and welcomed them. Unfortunately, her passive behavior during the meeting with the tenant association's subcommittee set a poor model for Judith to follow with her classmates.

Cindy was taking a risk in entering the study team's conversation. Judith probably felt a lack of respect from her mother—and if she felt that way, it is possible that the two study-team girls also sensed it. While they might have felt that Judith was "wimping" out, they didn't expect Judith's mother to confirm it. Cindy could have gotten the message across to Judith if she had waited until the other girls had left before raising the subject.

Cindy could also have participated in the study team's conversation about the assignment during dinner. She might have drawn them out and taught Judith, by example, how to be appropriately aggressive; that is, assertive, independent, and collaborative.

MOTIVATION

Each person lives in many social worlds—family, school, work, peer groups, religion, hobby groups. To enter and then to survive in these groups require a well-developed set of social skills. Some of the skills are taught by the groups. But many of the skills are first presented by parents who want their children to become responsible and respected members of their various communities.

TIMING

The basic teaching by parents of social skills starts at birth and continues until maturity. The day-to-day treatment of each other, of significant others, of adult peers, of authority figures, of all other people, shapes the behavior that children learn. It is the key part of their acquisition of social skills.

OPTIONS

Cindy needs to recognize—more than she already has—that she is the model for the social skills being learned by Judith. Among her options is to step back and think about how her actions are likely to be perceived by Judith. In many ways, adolescent children are like sponges, acquiring knowledge and experiences quickly, and often, in a haphazard fashion without understanding. Cindy's role is to try to proffer those experiences in ways that Judith can understand and will accept, and from which she will learn.

BENEFITS

Parents who interact with and learn more about their child's friends are in a better position to guide their child in establishing and maintaining peer relationships. Negative peer groups are less likely to attract youngsters whose parents are respected by their friends.

Judith is aware when Cindy acts hypocritically. She seems to delight in determining whether Cindy practices what she preaches—particularly in peer relationships. This can have a positive side; it encourages Cindy to be at her best in interactions. Inviting children into the interaction, especially when positive, and telling them about positive interactions, help them to understand more about adult peer relationships. In turn, this knowledge can be transferred to their own peer relationships.

Encouraging Independent Thinking

Grandma and Grandpa Young are coming to visit. Every year, after the holidays, they come to visit and stay for about two weeks in January. During previous visits, Jason has given up his room for two weeks and slept in the den. Now, as a junior in high school, he is facing exams shortly and needs the time and privacy to study.

When the dates of the grandparents' visit are confirmed, Jason's parents assume that he will again move into the den to accommodate his grandparents. Jason reacts angrily and questions, "Why me?" He wonders why not his younger sister, Andrea, or his parents.

His parents answer, "We've always done it this way and see no reason to change."

Jason says, "I need to study for my exams. You want me to get good grades so I can get into a good college and maybe even qualify for a scholarship. Now you speak out of both sides of your mouths. You didn't ask me to move—you ordered me and that isn't fair. Maybe I could come up with a better solution."

Jason's parents are taken aback but say, "Let's talk about this tomorrow evening. You can offer any ideas you like to solve the problem."

The next evening, Jason proposes: 1.) asking his grandparents to wait two weeks before coming so that his exams would be over; 2.) asking Grandma to share Andrea's room and Grandpa to share his room; 3.) asking that his father and he build a temporary partition to close off the den for the grand-parents to use during their stay.

Jason barely finishes reporting his ideas before his parents reject them. "Your ideas are not reasonable. In fact, they are off the wall."

Jason asks, "Can't we even discuss this with Grandma and Grandpa?"

"No way. They will be treated as honored guests by all of us and that, young man, includes you."

Jason reacts, "How am I to believe you when you say you really want to hear my ideas?" Andrea hears the entire interaction. Above all, she is thankful that no one will be invading her room.

ACTION

Jason's parents haven't accepted new ideas from Jason, nor are they encouraging him to think independently. They are not helping him think through which of several ways of dealing with a problem would work best. They haven't even helped him to see that the problem involves not only their household but also the grandparents. Jason has served notice that he feels uncomfortable about sharing ideas and feelings with them in the future. While youth will often disagree with parents, just for the sake of disagreeing, Jason had a good reason—he wants to prepare for his exams and proposed some reasonable solutions. With Jason under school pressure, and the parents feeling pressure from the impending visit, emotions need to be calmed to improve problem solving.

Since the grandparents are scheduled to arrive in about six weeks, there is some time to try to work out the problem and to talk it over with the grandparents.

The parents' actions won't encourage Jason to think of novel solutions to problems, nor will it allow him to disagree when he believes he has a better idea that might work. Jason has warned them of a potential future problem—he doesn't believe they will listen to any of his ideas. In turn, he might not listen to any of theirs.

MOTIVATION

Most parents are aware that their children need to learn to solve their own problems as they mature. Providing solutions to their children's problems keeps the children dependent upon parents and also retards the social, mental, and emotional growth of the children. Independent thinking expands as a result of trial and error, making mistakes. Older children can think abstractly and can avoid some hard lessons in life by imagining the outcomes of various actions and by thinking through the likely consequences. Parents who encourage their children to think independently also teach by sharing the decision-making and taking prudent risks in unorthodox thinking. A shared error or realization of a likely error helps to teach. Assigning blame discourages learning.

TIMING

Experiential learning requires time and a clear head. It requires calming of emotions, the time to think, plan, try, succeed or fail, and to start over. Youth tends to be impatient. However, parents can't afford that luxury in dealing with their children. Parents who can deliberately slow the speed of their reactions to children's thinking and ideas will usually do better at solving problems, maintaining relationships, and teaching their children to think independently.

OPTIONS

A minimal parental response to Jason's ideas should have been, "Give me a day or two to think about it. I need to think through how it might work. Thanks." Another response, which begins the process of evaluating alternatives, might have been, "Would just sharing your room with Grandpa give you enough privacy to study?" Or, "What might Grandpa and Grandma want?" Instead of rejecting Jason's ideas, there could have been a reasonable discussion about the costs and effects of each alternative. Together, they might have generated even more alternatives.

BENEFITS

Parents who learn to accept a child's new ideas will discover that their parental roles will change over time. They will move from being authority figures who judge good and bad, to becoming coaches and counselors who teach independent thinking. The move also includes gradually relinquishing control over the children's lives while training them to think independently.

Treating Children as Equals

Whenever the family gets into the car for a trip—whether long or short—there is an argument over the type of music that gets played on the CD player. As a trip begins, Steve, who is thirteen years old, tells his parents about a classroom discussion involving musical artists. The class concluded that "all fathers like Bob Dylan." Steve likes the bands Green Day or Offspring. His eleven-year-old sister, Heather, likes the Spice Girls.

Steve teases his father by saying, "I guess you have to be real old to like that kind of music. It's so slow and dreary. I can't stay awake when I hear it. So go ahead, Dad, you can play it on the trip. Just be careful you don't fall asleep at the wheel."

For Steve's father, it is one thing to argue about who will use the CD player for how long, and quite another to be classified as an "old man" by your son in front of your wife and daughter. He responds angrily, "What do you know? When I want to hear any of that loud, annoying music, I'll tell you. That music rattles your brains. When was the last time you read a newspaper? If my tastes bother you because I am 'old,' then your taste in music bothers me because you are young and immature."

Steve answers, "Gee, Dad, I was only teasing. You don't have to get so angry." Heather has witnessed the exchange and is puzzled. She wonders if Steve has overstepped his bounds by teasing his father.

ACTION

Steve's father did not react well to being told he was "old." With Heather listening, the father verbally struck out at Steve by questioning his maturity, taste, and choice of activities. While children often tease cruelly and harshly, the father could have handled Steve's teasing in a more positive way. He could have exhibited a more gentle form of interaction. He might have given a more positive spin to the term "old" . . . such as "classic." He could have directed the conversation back to developing a way of honoring everyone's musical choices. Little was accomplished by attacking Steve and questioning his taste in music and the frequency of reading a newspaper.

As the environment became calmer, the whole family might have sought agreement on a music-listening strategy. Maybe a portable CD player with earphones could be purchased so that Steve or his father—when not driving—could privately listen to his preferred music. Or, a schedule for listening, including an agreement on volume control, might also have helped. The father needs to be aware that every action taken with regard to Steve has an impact on Heather. As she matures, there is a need to include her in the discussions and begin treating her as an equal.

MOTIVATION

Children are their parents' equals in many areas. First and foremost, they are separate human beings with inherent worth and dignity. Honest interchange acknowledges children's positive qualities and abilities. The family, or household, is also one of the first places children learn about diversity . . . in size, power, needs, age, interests, roles, tastes, characteristics, and abilities.

TIMING

The child is *not always* the parent's equal. A mental inventory of those areas where the child comes close to being your equal will help you decide when to treat your child accordingly. Children detect hypocrisy in others quite rapidly. A parent who talks down to a child, or falsely acts as if the child were equal, is hypocritical. The results of hypocrisy will not include fostering a perception of love.

OPTIONS

Both parents and children benefit from working out—in the safety and intimacy of the family—ways of dealing with differences in music preference and other diversities. Common tactics are humor, taking turns, sharing, and division of labor based on competencies. Treating others appropriately as equals is respectful of diversity. Both parents and children learn they can be enriched by diversity. To be blunt, unless we let ourselves hear a different opinion, we are always left only talking to ourselves.

BENEFITS

As children mature, they progressively seek greater mastery, greater skill, more independence, and more control over their own lives. While there are benchmarks to indicate that growth in various areas is being achieved, there is no magic event or single occurrence to signal "adulthood" or "maturity." One clear sign of achieving maturity is being treated as an equal by parents and other adults. This enhances children's self-esteem and reinforces their ability to undertake new experiences and take prudent risks.

CHAPTER 7

MEASURE YOUR PRETEEN'S PERCEPTION OF LOVE

Until now in this book, we have talked about children's perception of love in a general way. That is, we have seen how certain principles apply in situations involving *other* people, *other* people's children.

It's time now to bring these principles closer to home. It is time to try to answer the question that we began with: *Do your kids know you love them?*

How do the concepts in this book relate to my children and me?

If you're like a lot of parents, you have probably spent some time measuring yourself against our discussions of communication styles, parenting styles, and the five elements of the perception of love. You have probably been pleased with your parenting skills in some areas and not so pleased in others. You may even feel that you have done an excellent job of letting your children know you love them.

But we ask you to stop right here. We ask you to stop and remember the crucial, pivotal point that we are trying to make: **It is not what the *parent believes* that matters. It is what the *child perceives* that makes the difference.**

The following test is designed for parents of young children (generally age twelve or younger) to help you discover their perception of love from you. (A similar test to be taken by adolescents follows in Chapter 8.) You will be asked to answer the questions *as you believe your child would answer.*

At the end of this chapter, we offer a method of analyzing the information to provide a benchmark for your child's current perception of love. There are separate tests for the mother and the father. These tests should be analyzed separately without comparing the two parents.

Mothers

1. Read each question carefully. There are 72 in all.
2. The questions require you to try to see things the way you think your child sees them. This is really tough because you are trying to visualize what you do as seen through the eyes of someone else—your child.
3. If you agree that the statement correctly describes the way you think your child would say you act *most of the time,* then check the "Yes" box.
4. If you think that your child believes you *do not* act that way *most of the time,* then check the "No" box.
5. The test is *only* about how you think that child sees you. Don't consider how your child sees anyone else or how anyone else sees you.
6. Do not discuss the answers with anyone while completing this test.

REMEMBER: DO YOU AGREE THAT THIS IS THE WAY YOUR CHILD *THINKS YOU ACT?*

1. Does your mother allow you to pick your own friends?
    Yes___ No___

2. Does your mother let you choose what you want to do whenever possible?
   Yes___ No___

3. Does your mother allow you to spend the money you earn in any way you pick?
   Yes___ No___

4. Does your mother let you plan your own schedule to do your chores?
   Yes___ No___

5. Does your mother let you decide what you will wear when you will be with your friends?
   Yes___ No___

6. Will your mother let you decide the colors to paint the walls of your bedroom?
   Yes___ No___

7. Does your mother enjoy having you bring your friends home?
   Yes___ No___

8. Does your mother let you have friends at home often?
   Yes___ No___

9. Do your friends respect your mother?
   Yes___ No___

10. Does your mother treat your friends with respect and courtesy?
    Yes___ No___

11. Does your mother include you in adult conversations with her friends and relatives?
    Yes___ No___

12. Does your mother try to meet your friends' parents?
    Yes___ No___

13. Can you tell your mother if you think your ideas are better than hers?
    Yes___ No___

14. Does your mother ask you how to do certain things?
    Yes___ No___

15. Does your mother like you to do things your own way?
    Yes___ No___

16. Does your mother prefer you to consider her ideas before making up your mind?
    Yes___ No___

17. Does your mother encourage you to both ask questions and to find answers?
    Yes___ No___

18. Does your mother encourage you to also consider unusual solutions to problems?
    Yes___ No___

19. Does your mother like to talk about things with you?
    Yes___ No___

20. Does your mother like for you to tease her occasionally about some things?
    Yes___ No___

21. Does your mother really want you to tell her about how you feel about things?
    Yes___ No___

22. Your mother doesn't talk down to you.
    Yes___ No___

23. Does your mother give you information to help make decisions but then won't order you around?
    Yes___ No___

24. Does your mother tease you as if you were an adult?
    Yes___ No___

25. Does your mother say that you are very good-natured?
    Yes___ No___

26. Is your mother happy to see you when you come home from school?
    Yes___ No___

27. Does your mother tell you that she's proud of you?
    Yes___ No___

28. Does your mother compliment you when you do something well?
    Yes___ No___

29. Does your mother speak more often of what you do well rather than the mistakes you make?
    Yes___ No___

30. Does your mother often praise you in front of other people?
    Yes___ No___

31. Does your mother enjoy talking things over with you?
    Yes___ No___

32. Does your mother enjoy doing things with you?
    Yes___ No___

33. Does your mother have a good time at home with you?
    Yes___ No___

34. Has your mother talked about her problems and her successes with you?
Yes___ No___

35. Does your mother talk about her childhood with you?
Yes___ No___

36. Does your mother enjoy teaching you how to use some of her personal things?
Yes___ No___

37. Does your mother mostly speak to you in a warm and friendly voice?
Yes___ No___

38. Does your mother often smile at you?
Yes___ No___

39. Does your mother tell you how much she loves you?
Yes___ No___

40. Does your mother kiss you on the cheek when she comes home?
Yes___ No___

41. Does your mother use warm and affectionate nicknames for you?
Yes___ No___

42. Does your mother tell you how much she misses you when you are away from each other?
Yes___ No___

43. Does your mother make you feel better if you talk over your worries with her?
Yes___ No___

44. Does your mother give you sympathy when you need it?
    Yes___ No___

45. Does your mother cheer you up when you are sad?
    Yes___ No___

46. Does your mother encourage you to keep working at solving a tough problem?
    Yes___ No___

47. Does your mother try to help you understand that there are both good times and bad times in life?
    Yes___ No___

48. Does your mother listen when you need someone to listen to you?
    Yes___ No___

49. Does your mother encourage you to read?
    Yes___ No___

50. Does your mother help you find out more about things that are important to you?
    Yes___ No___

51. Does your mother talk with you about science?
    Yes___ No___

52. Does your mother help you to make things?
    Yes___ No___

53. Does your mother play games with you that make you think a lot?
    Yes___ No___

54. Does your mother encourage you to learn about computers?
    Yes___ No___

55. Does your mother often give up something to be able to get something for you?
     Yes___   No___

56. Does your mother make you feel like the most important person in her life?
     Yes___   No___

57. Does your mother give you a lot of care and attention?
     Yes___   No___

58. Does your mother do things with you that she knows you like doing?
     Yes___   No___

59. Is your mother concerned that you have a good time when you do things together?
     Yes___   No___

60. Does your mother consider your needs before her own?
     Yes___   No___

61. Does your mother like you to spend a lot of your free time at home?
     Yes___   No___

62. Does your mother seem to be sorry you are growing up?
     Yes___   No___

63. Does your mother allow you much time to yourself?
     Yes___   No___

64. Does your mother seem to feel hurt if you want to do things alone?
     Yes___   No___

65. Does your mother want you to be like her when she was in school?
     Yes___   No___

66. Does your mother want you to grow up to be just like her?
    Yes___ No___

67. Does your mother worry about your health?
    Yes___ No___

68. Does your mother worry that something might happen to you?
    Yes___ No___

69. Does your mother work hard to prevent you from failing at something you want to do?
    Yes___ No___

70. Is your mother concerned about your playing some sports because they could be dangerous?
    Yes___ No___

71. Is your mother very careful about the kinds of friends you choose?
    Yes___ No___

72. Does your mother make sure that you follow the rules and stay out of trouble?
    Yes___ No___

You have completed the test.

Scoring Mother

Number of Questions Answered

Questions	Domain	Yes	No	Action Required?
1 to 6	*Moderate Freedom*	___	___	_____
7 to 12	*Encourage Sociability*	___	___	_____
13 to 18	*Enc. Indep. Thinking*	___	___	_____
19 to 24	*Equal Treatment*	___	___	_____
25 to 30	*Positive Evaluation*	___	___	_____
31 to 36	*Sharing*	___	___	_____
37 to 42	*Expressing Affection*	___	___	_____
43 to 48	*Emotional Support*	___	___	_____
49 to 54	*Intellectual Stimulation*	___	___	_____
55 to 60	*Being Child-Centered*	___	___	_____
61 to 66	*Possessiveness*	___	___	_____
67 to 72	*Protectiveness*	___	___	_____

STEP 1 *Using YOUR own test, count the number of "Yes" answers for each set of six questions. Enter that count in the "Yes" column for the set of six question numbers shown. Also, count the number of "No" answers for each set of six questions and enter that count in the "No" column.*

STEP 2 *On the scoring sheet, locate any domain (row) where the number of "Yes" answers is 5 or 6. For any row where the number of "Yes" answers is 5 or 6, write "NONE" under the column "ACTION REQUIRED?"*

STEP 3 *On the scoring sheet above, locate any domain (row) where the number of "No" answers is 5 or 6. For any row where the number of "No" answers is 5 or 6, write "MAJOR" under the column "ACTION REQUIRED?"*

STEP 4 *On the scoring sheet, identify the remaining rows which do not have any entry under "ACTION REQUIRED?" For those rows, enter "MINOR" under "ACTION REQUIRED?"*

See example below:

Number of Questions Answered

Questions	Domain	Yes	No	Action Required?
1 to 6	*Moderate Freedom*	6	0	NONE
7 to 12	*Encourage Sociability*	6	0	NONE
13 to 18	*Enc. Indep. Thinking*	3	3	MINOR
19 to 24	*Equal Treatment*	2	4	MINOR
25 to 30	*Positive Evaluation*	1	5	MAJOR
31 to 36	*Sharing*	5	1	NONE
37 to 42	*Expressing Affection*	1	5	MAJOR
43 to 48	*Emotional Support*	5	1	NONE
49 to 54	*Intellectual Stimulation*	5	1	NONE
55 to 60	*Being Child-Centered*	4	2	MINOR
61 to 66	*Possessiveness*	2	3	MINOR
67 to 72	*Protectiveness*	6	0	NONE

The scoring and analysis of this example shows:

The parent who completed this test believes that his/her child is perceiving love in the following domains and that **no action is required to improve that perception.**

> *Moderate freedom*
> *Encouraging socialibility*
> *Sharing*
> *Emotional Support*
> *Intellectual Stimulation*
> *Protectiveness*

The parent who completed this test believes that his/her child is perceiving some love in the following domains and that **some action is required to improve that perception.**

Encouraging Independent Thinking
Equal Treatment
Being Child-Centered
Possessiveness

The parent who completed this test believes that his/her child is **NOT perceiving love in the following domains and major action is required by the parent to improve that perception.**

Positive Evaluation
Expressing Affection

This completes the Preliminary Analysis. The parent now has benchmark information indicating those domains where he or she believes the child is perceiving much love, some love, or no love at all.

Fathers

1. Read each question carefully. There are 72 in all.
2. The questions require you to try to see things the way you think your child sees them. This is really tough because you are trying to visualize what you do as seen through the eyes of someone else—your child.
3. If you agree that the statement correctly describes the way you think your child would say you act *most of the time,* then check the "Yes" box.
4. If you think that your child believes you *do not* act that way *most of the time,* then check the "No" box.
5. The test is *only* about how you think that child sees you. Don't consider how your child sees anyone else or how anyone else sees you.
6. Do not discuss the answers with anyone while completing this test.

REMEMBER: DO YOU AGREE THAT THIS IS THE WAY YOUR CHILD *THINKS YOU ACT*?

1. Does your father allow you to pick your own friends?
   Yes___ No___

2. Does your father let you choose what you want to do whenever possible?
   Yes___ No___

3. Does your father allow you to spend the money you earn in any way you pick?
   Yes___ No___

4. Does your father let you plan your own schedule to do your chores?
   Yes___ No___

5. Does your father let you decide what you will wear when you will be with your friends?
   Yes___ No___

6. Will your father let you decide the colors to paint the walls of your bedroom?
   Yes___ No___

7. Does your father enjoy having you bring your friends home?
   Yes___ No___

8. Does your father let you have friends at home often?
   Yes___ No___

9. Do your friends respect your father?
   Yes___ No___

10. Does your father treat your friends with respect and courtesy?
    Yes___ No___

11. Does your father include you in adult conversations with his friends and relatives?
    Yes___ No___

12. Does your father try to meet your friends' parents?
    Yes___ No___

13. Can you tell your father if you think your ideas are better than his?
    Yes___ No___

14. Does your father ask you how to do certain things?
    Yes___ No___

15. Does your father like you to do things your own way?
    Yes___ No___

16. Does your father prefer you to consider his ideas before making up your mind?
    Yes___ No___

17. Does your father encourage you to both ask questions and to find answers?
    Yes___ No___

18. Does your father encourage you to also consider unusual solutions to problems?
    Yes___ No___

19. Does your father like to talk about things with you?
    Yes___ No___

20. Does your father like for you to tease him occasionally about some things?
    Yes___ No___

21. Does your father really want you to tell him about how you feel about things?
    Yes___ No___

22. Your father doesn't talk down to you.
     Yes___ No___

23. Does your father give you information to help make decisions but then won't order you around?
     Yes___ No___

24. Does your father tease you as if you were an adult?
     Yes___ No___

25. Does your father say that you are very good-natured?
     Yes___ No___

26. Does your father often praise you?
     Yes___ No___

27. Does your father tell you that he's proud of you?
     Yes___ No___

28. Does your father compliment you when you do something well?
     Yes___ No___

29. Does your father speak more often of what you do well rather than of the mistakes you make?
     Yes___ No___

30. Does your father often praise you in front of other people?
     Yes___ No___

31. Does your father enjoy talking things over with you?
     Yes___ No___

32. Does your father enjoy doing things with you?
     Yes___ No___

33. Does your father have a good time at home with you?
     Yes___ No___

34. Has your father talked about his problems and his successes with you?
    Yes___ No___

35. Does your father talk about his childhood with you?
    Yes___ No___

36. Does your father enjoy teaching you how to use some of his personal things?
    Yes___ No___

37. Does your father mostly speak to you in a warm and friendly voice?
    Yes___ No___

38. Does your father often smile at you?
    Yes___ No___

39. Does your father tell you that he loves you?
    Yes___ No___

40. Does your father embrace or hug you when he comes home?
    Yes___ No___

41. Does your father use warm and affectionate nicknames for you?
    Yes___ No___

42. Does your father tell you how much he misses you when you are away from each other?
    Yes___ No___

43. Does your father make you feel better if you talk over your worries with him?
    Yes___ No___

44. Does your father give you sympathy when you need it?
    Yes___ No___

45. Does your father cheer you up when you are sad?
    Yes___ No___

46. Does your father encourage you to keep working at solving a tough problem?
    Yes___ No___

47. Does your father try to help you understand that there are both good times and bad times in life?
    Yes___ No___

48. Does your father listen when you need someone to listen to you?
    Yes___ No___

49. Does your father encourage you to read?
    Yes___ No___

50. Does your father help you find out more about things that are important to you?
    Yes___ No___

51. Does your father talk with you about science?
    Yes___ No___

52. Does your father help you to make things?
    Yes___ No___

53. Does your father play games with you that make you think a lot?
    Yes___ No___

54. Does your father encourage you to learn about computers?
    Yes___ No___

55. Does your father often give up something to be able to get something for you?
    Yes___ No___

56. Does your father make you feel like the most important person in his life?
    Yes___ No___

57. Does your father give you a lot of care and attention?
    Yes___ No___

58. Does your father do things with you that he knows you like doing?
    Yes___ No___

59. Is your father concerned that you have a good time when you do things together?
    Yes___ No___

60. Does your father consider your needs before his own?
    Yes___ No___

61. Does your father like you to spend a lot of your free time at home?
    Yes___ No___

62. Does your father seem to be sorry you are growing up?
    Yes___ No___

63. Does your father allow you much time to yourself?
    Yes___ No___

64. Does your father seem to feel hurt if you want to do things alone?
    Yes___ No___

65. Does your father want you to be like him when he was in school?
    Yes___ No___

66. Does your father want you to grow up to be just like him?
    Yes___ No___

67. Does your father worry about your health?
    Yes___ No___

68. Does your father worry that something might happen to you?
    Yes___ No___

69. Does your father work hard to prevent you from failing at something you want to do?
    Yes___ No___

70. Is your father concerned about your playing some sports because they could be dangerous?
    Yes___ No___

71. Is your father very careful about the kinds of friends you choose?
    Yes___ No___

72. Does your father make sure that you follow the rules and stay out of trouble?
    Yes___ No___

You have completed the test.

Scoring Father

Number of Questions Answered

Questions	Domain	Yes	No	Action Required?
1 to 6	*Moderate Freedom*	___	___	_____
7 to 12	*Encourage Sociability*	___	___	_____
13 to 18	*Enc. Indep. Thinking*	___	___	_____
19 to 24	*Equal Treatment*	___	___	_____
25 to 30	*Positive Evaluation*	___	___	_____
31 to 36	*Sharing*	___	___	_____
37 to 42	*Expressing Affection*	___	___	_____
43 to 48	*Emotional Support*	___	___	_____
49 to 54	*Intellectual Stimulation*	___	___	_____
55 to 60	*Being Child-Centered*	___	___	_____
61 to 66	*Possessiveness*	___	___	_____
67 to 72	*Protectiveness*	___	___	_____

STEP 1 *Using YOUR own test, count the number of "Yes" answers for each set of six questions. Enter that count in the "Yes" column for the set of six question numbers shown. Also, count the number of "No" answers for each set of six questions and enter that count in the "No" column.*

STEP 2 *On the scoring sheet, locate any domain (row) where the number of "Yes" answers is 5 or 6. For any row where the number of "Yes" answers is 5 or 6, write "NONE" under the column "ACTION REQUIRED?"*

STEP 3 *On the scoring sheet above, locate any domain (row) where the number of "No" answers is 5 or 6. For any row where the number of "No" answers is 5 or 6, write "MAJOR" under the column "ACTION REQUIRED?"*

STEP 4 *On the scoring sheet, identify the remaining rows which do* *not have any entry under "ACTION REQUIRED?" For those rows, enter "MINOR" under "ACTION REQUIRED?"*

See example below:

Number of Questions Answered

Questions	Domain	Yes	No	Action Required?
1 to 6	*Moderate Freedom*	6	0	NONE
7 to 12	*Encourage Sociability*	6	0	NONE
13 to 18	*Enc. Indep. Thinking*	3	3	MINOR
19 to 24	*Equal Treatment*	2	4	MINOR
25 to 30	*Positive Evaluation*	1	5	MAJOR
31 to 36	*Sharing*	5	1	NONE
37 to 42	*Expressing Affection*	1	5	MAJOR
43 to 48	*Emotional Support*	5	1	NONE
49 to 54	*Intellectual Stimulation*	5	1	NONE
55 to 60	*Being Child-Centered*	4	2	MINOR
61 to 66	*Possessiveness*	3	3	MINOR
67 to 72	*Protectiveness*	6	0	NONE

The scoring and analysis of this example shows:

The parent who completed this test believes that his/her child is perceiving love in the following domains and that **no action is required to improve that perception.**

Moderate freedom
Encouraging socialibility
Sharing
Emotional Support
Intellectual Stimulation
Protectiveness

The parent who completed this test believes that his/her child is perceiving some love in the following domains and that **some action is required to improve that perception.**

> *Encouraging Independent Thinking*
> *Equal Treatment*
> *Being Child-Centered*
> *Possessiveness*

The parent who completed this test believes that his/her child is **NOT perceiving love in the following domains and major action is required by the parent to improve that perception.**

> *Positive Evaluation*
> *Expressing Affection*

This completes the Preliminary Analysis. The parent now has benchmark information indicating those domains where he or she believes the child is perceiving much love, some love, or no love at all.

CHAPTER 8

MEASURE YOUR ADOLESCENT'S PERCEPTION OF LOVE

Today's adolescent is neither a fully matured adult in a developing body nor a larger version of an immature child. Once in puberty, the child changes at an amazing rate. At times, it seems as if this adolescent being is trying on a new physical body to see if it will fit—and most of the time, it doesn't. At the same time, the mind is being bombarded with a new energy emanating from hormonal changes that require it to think differently than ever before.

Suddenly, adolescents are capable of thinking abstractly. They are now capable of thinking about *why* they are thinking *about what* they are thinking. And, they are now capable of trying to understand love—love from their parents, love to their parents, and love relationships among their peers.

In this chapter we will be examining adolescents' perception of love from their parents. We will be comparing those actual adolescent perceptions to what their parents believe the adolescents are perceiving (which we measured, using the tests in Chapter 7).

If your child has not yet entered adolescence, please take

the test in Chapter 7, then continue on to Chapter 9 Do not use the tests in this chapter.

This chapter contains the forms and procedures to compare the test answers between parent and adolescent and analyze the results creating a benchmark for progress. In this chapter, we have provided sufficient test and analysis forms for two parents—MOTHER and FATHER and one of their children. The adolescent will have to complete two versions of the test—one to assess the behavior of each of the parents toward the adolescent. *If the parent(s) wish to repeat the testing and analysis for more than one adolescent, they should duplicate the tests.* If the additional child or children are not yet adolescents, turn to Chapter 7 and use the tests and methods in it.

There are separate tests for mother and father. When we say "Mother," we mean the primary female caregiver. Similarly, "Father" is interpreted to mean the primary male caregiver.

If you are a single parent, complete only one test for each adolescent. There are sufficient test copies for the single parent to examine the perceptions for two children. If two parents are participating, both should select and answer questions about the same adolescent.

ADOLESCENTS (ABOUT MOTHERS)

1. Read each question carefully. There are 72 in all.
2. If you agree that the statement correctly describes the way you think your mother acts *most of the time* toward you, then check the "Yes" box.
3. If you think that your mother *does not* act that way *most of the time,* then check the "No" box.
4. The test is *only* about how you think your mother acts toward you. Don't consider how your mother acts toward anyone else or how anyone else acts toward you.
5. Do not discuss the answers with anyone while completing this test.

REMEMBER: DO YOU AGREE THAT THIS IS THE WAY YOU BELIEVE YOUR MOTHER ACTS TOWARD YOU?

1. Does your mother allow you to pick your own friends?
   Yes __   No __

2. Does your mother let you choose what you want to do whenever possible?
   Yes __   No __

3. Does your mother allow you to spend the money you earn in any way you pick?
   Yes __   No __

4. Does your mother let you plan your own schedule to do your chores?
   Yes __   No __

5. Does your mother let you decide what you will wear when you will be with your friends?
   Yes __   No __

6. Will your mother let you decide the colors to paint the walls of your bedroom?
   Yes __   No __

7. Does your mother enjoy having you bring your friends home?
   Yes __   No __

8. Does your mother let you have friends at home often?
   Yes __   No __

9. Do your friends respect your mother?
   Yes __   No __

10. Does your mother treat your friends with respect and courtesy?
    Yes __   No __

11. Does your mother include you in adult conversations with her friends and relatives?
    Yes __   No __

12. Does your mother try to meet your friends' parents?
    Yes __   No __

13. Can you tell your mother if you think your ideas are better than hers?
    Yes __   No __

14. Does your mother ask you how to do certain things?
    Yes __   No __

15. Does your mother like you to do things your own way?
    Yes __   No __

16. Does your mother prefer you to consider her ideas before making up your mind?
    Yes __   No __

17. Does your mother encourage you to both ask questions and to find answers?
    Yes __   No __

18. Does your mother encourage you to also consider unusual solutions to problems?
    Yes __   No __

19. Does your mother like to talk about things with you?
    Yes __   No __

20. Does your mother like for you to tease her occasionally about some things?
    Yes __ No __

21. Does your mother really want you to tell her about how you feel about things?
    Yes __ No __

22. Your mother doesn't talk down to you.
    Yes __ No __

23. Does your mother give you information to help make decisions but then won't order you around?
    Yes __ No __

24. Does your mother tease you as if you were an adult?
    Yes __ No __

25. Does your mother say that you are very good-natured?
    Yes __ No __

26. Is your mother happy to see you when you come home from school?
    Yes __ No __

27. Does your mother tell you that she's proud of you?
    Yes __ No __

28. Does your mother compliment you when you do something well?
    Yes __ No __

29. Does your mother speak more often of what you do well rather than of the mistakes you make?
    Yes __ No __

30. Does your mother often praise you in front of other people?
    Yes __   No __

31. Does your mother enjoy talking things over with you?
    Yes __   No __

32. Does your mother enjoy doing things with you?
    Yes __   No __

33. Does your mother have a good time at home with you?
    Yes __   No __

34. Has your mother talked about her problems and her successes with you?
    Yes __   No __

35. Does your mother talk about her childhood with you?
    Yes __   No __

36. Does your mother enjoy teaching you how to use some of her personal things?
    Yes __   No __

37. Does your mother mostly speak to you in a warm and friendly voice?
    Yes __   No __

38. Does your mother often smile at you?
    Yes __   No __

39. Does your mother tell you how much she loves you?
    Yes __   No __

40. Does your mother kiss you on the cheek when she comes home?
    Yes __   No __

41. Does your mother use warm and affectionate nicknames for you?
    Yes __ No __

42. Does your mother tell you how much she misses you when you are away from each other?
    Yes __ No __

43. Does your mother make you feel better if you talk over your worries with her?
    Yes __ No __

44. Does your mother give you sympathy when you need it?
    Yes __ No __

45. Does your mother cheer you up when you are sad?
    Yes __ No __

46. Does your mother encourage you to keep working at solving a tough problem?
    Yes __ No __

47. Does your mother try to help you understand that there are both good times and bad times in life?
    Yes __ No __

48. Does your mother listen when you need someone to listen to you?
    Yes __ No __

49. Does your mother encourage you to read?
    Yes __ No __

50. Does your mother help you find out more about things that are important to you?
    Yes __ No __

51. Does your mother talk with you about science?
Yes __ No __

52. Does your mother help you to make things?
Yes __ No __

53. Does your mother play games with you that make you think a lot?
Yes __ No __

54. Does your mother encourage you to learn about computers?
Yes __ No __

55. Does your mother often give up something to be able to get something for you?
Yes __ No __

56. Does your mother make you feel like the most important person in her life?
Yes __ No __

57. Does your mother give you a lot of care and attention?
Yes __ No __

58. Does your mother do things with you that she knows you like doing?
Yes __ No __

59. Is your mother concerned that you have a good time when you do things together?
Yes __ No __

60. Does your mother consider your needs before her own?
Yes __ No __

61. Does your mother like you to spend a lot of your free time at home?
    Yes __ No __

62. Does your mother seem to be sorry you are growing up?
    Yes __ No __

63. Does your mother allow you much time to yourself?
    Yes __ No __

64. Does your mother seem to feel hurt if you want to do things alone?
    Yes __ No __

65. Does your mother want you to be like her when she was in school?
    Yes __ No __

66. Does your mother want you to grow up to be just like her?
    Yes __ No __

67. Does your mother worry about your health?
    Yes __ No __

68. Does your mother worry that something might happen to you?
    Yes __ No __

69. Does your mother work hard to prevent you from failing at something you want to do?
    Yes __ No __

70. Is your mother concerned about your playing some sports because they could be dangerous?
    Yes __ No __

71. Is your mother very careful about the kinds of friends you choose?

    Yes ___ No ___

72. Does your mother make sure that you follow the rules and stay out of trouble?

    Yes ___ No

You have completed the test.

ADOLESCENTS (ABOUT FATHERS)

1. Read each question carefully. There are 72 in all.
2. If you agree that the statement correctly describes the way you think your father acts *most of the time* toward you, then check the "Yes" box.
3. If you think that your father *does not* act that way *most of the time*, then check the "No" box.
4. The test is *only* about how you think your father acts toward you. Don't consider how your father acts toward anyone else or how anyone else acts toward you.
5. Do not discuss the answers with anyone while completing this test.

REMEMBER: DO YOU AGREE THAT THIS IS THE WAY YOU BELIEVE YOUR FATHER ACTS TOWARD YOU?

1. Does your father allow you to pick your own friends?

    Yes ___ No ___

2. Does your father let you choose what you want to do whenever possible?

    Yes ___ No ___

3. Does your father allow you to spend the money you earn in any way you pick?

    Yes ___ No ___

4. Does your father let you plan your own schedule to do your chores?
   Yes __ No __

5. Does your father let you decide what you will wear when you will be with your friends?
   Yes __ No __

6. Will your father let you decide the colors to paint the walls of your bedroom?
   Yes __ No __

7. Does your father enjoy having you bring your friends home?
   Yes __ No __

8. Does your father let you have friends at home often?
   Yes __ No __

9. Do your friends respect your father?
   Yes __ No __

10. Does your father treat your friends with respect and courtesy?
    Yes __ No __

11. Does your father include you in adult conversations with his friends and relatives?
    Yes __ No __

12. Does your father try to meet your friends' parents?
    Yes __ No __

13. Can you tell your father if you think your ideas are better than his?
    Yes __ No __

14. Does your father ask you how to do certain things?
    Yes __ No __

15. Does your father like you to do things your own way?
    Yes __ No __

16. Does your father prefer you to consider his ideas before making up your mind?
    Yes __ No __

17. Does your father encourage you to both ask questions and to find answers?
    Yes __ No __

18. Does your father encourage you to also consider unusual solutions to problems?
    Yes __ No __

19. Does your father like to talk about things with you?
    Yes __ No __

20. Does your father like for you to tease him occasionally about some things?
    Yes __ No __

21. Does your father really want you to tell him about how you feel about things?
    Yes __ No __

22. Your father doesn't talk down to you.
    Yes __ No __

23. Does your father give you information to help make decisions but then won't order you around?
    Yes __ No __

24. Does your father tease you as if you were an adult?
    Yes __ No __

25. Does your father say that you are very good-natured?
Yes __ No __

26. Does your father often praise you?
Yes __ No __

27. Does your father tell you that he's proud of you?
Yes __ No __

28. Does your father compliment you when you do something well?
Yes __ No __

29. Does your father speak more often of what you do well rather than of the mistakes you make?
Yes __ No __

30. Does your father often praise you in front of other people?
Yes __ No __

31. Does your father enjoy talking things over with you?
Yes __ No __

32. Does your father enjoy doing things with you?
Yes __ No __

33. Does your father have a good time at home with you?
Yes __ No __

34. Has your father talked about his problems and his successes with you?
Yes __ No __

35. Does your father talk about his childhood with you?
Yes __ No __

36. Does your father enjoy teaching you how to use some of his personal things?
    Yes __ No __

37. Does your father mostly speak to you in a warm and friendly voice?
    Yes __ No __

38. Does your father often smile at you?
    Yes __ No __

39. Does your father tell you how much he loves you?
    Yes __ No __

40. Does your father embrace or hug you when he comes home?
    Yes __ No __

41. Does your father use warm and affectionate nicknames for you?
    Yes __ No __

42. Does your father tell you how much he misses you when you are away from each other?
    Yes __ No __

43. Does your father make you feel better if you talk over your worries with him?
    Yes __ No __

44. Does your father give you sympathy when you need it?
    Yes __ No __

45. Does your father cheer you up when you are sad?
    Yes __ No __

46. Does your father encourage you to keep working at solving a tough problem?
    Yes __ No __

47. Does your father try to help you understand that there are both good times and bad times in life?
    Yes __ No __

48. Does your father listen when you need someone to listen to you?
    Yes __ No __

49. Does your father encourage you to read?
    Yes __ No __

50. Does your father help you find out more about things that are important to you?
    Yes __ No __

51. Does your father talk with you about science?
    Yes __ No __

52. Does your father help you to make things?
    Yes __ No __

53. Does your father play games with you that make you think a lot?
    Yes __ No __

54. Does your father encourage you to learn about computers?
    Yes __ No __

55. Does your father often give up something to be able to get something for you?
    Yes __ No __

56. Does your father make you feel like the most important person in his life?
Yes __ No __

57. Does your father give you a lot of care and attention?
Yes __ No __

58. Does your father do things with you that he knows you like doing?
Yes __ No __

59. Is your father concerned that you have a good time when you do things together?
Yes __ No __

60. Does your father consider your needs before his own?
Yes __ No __

61. Does your father like you to spend a lot of your free time at home?
Yes __ No __

62. Does your father seem to be sorry you are growing up?
Yes __ No __

63. Does your father allow you much time to yourself?
Yes __ No __

64. Does your father seem to feel hurt if you want to do things alone?
Yes __ No __

65. Does your father want you to be like him when he was in school?
Yes __ No __

66. Does your father want you to grow up to be just like him?
Yes __ No __

67. Does your father worry about your health?
    Yes __ No __

68. Does your father worry that something might happen to you?
    Yes __ No __

69. Does your father work hard to prevent you from failing at something you want to do?
    Yes __ No __

70. Is your father concerned about your playing some sports because they could be dangerous?
    Yes __ No __

71. Is your father very careful about the kinds of friends you choose?
    Yes __ No __

72. Does your father make sure that you follow the rules and stay out of trouble?
    Yes __ No __

You have completed the test. On the following pages your parent or parents will compare the tests they've taken with you.

Scoring

The tests you and your child have taken contain the same number of questions. Now you will compare your answers question by question, first Mom, then Dad.

Step 1 *Examine the answers to each question asked of both the adolescent and parent. If both checked "Yes" for Question #1, place a check under the column "Both Yes" for Question #1. If both checked "No" for Question #1, place a check under the column "Both No" for Question #1. If one checked "Yes" and the other checked "No," place a check under the column for "Yes/No."*

Step 2 *For each set of six questions, count the number of checks in each column and enter the number in the space "Totals" in each column. Copy these totals to the "Summary Scoring Sheet" at the row (domain) for those question numbers.*

Step 3 *Using the Summary Scoring Sheet, locate any domain (row) where—*

Both Yes–total is 5 or 6. For these rows, write "NONE" under the column "Action Required?"

Both No–total is 5 or 6. For these rows, write "MAJOR" under the column "Action Required?"

Yes/No–total is 5 or 6. For these rows, write "MAJOR" under the column "Action Required?"

Identify the remaining rows which do not have any entry under "ACTION REQUIRED?" For those rows, enter "MINOR" under "ACTION REQUIRED?"

Parent/Adolescent Test Comparison—Mother

Question #	Yes/No	Both Yes	Both No
1	—	—	—
2	—	—	—
3	—	—	—
4	—	—	—
5	—	—	—
6	—	—	—
TOTALS	——	——	——

Question #	Yes/No	Both Yes	Both No
7	——	——	——
8	——	——	——
9	——	——	——
10	——	——	——
11	——	——	——
12	——	——	——
TOTALS	——————	—————	—————

Question #	Yes/No	Both Yes	Both No
13	——	——	——
14	——	——	——
15	——	——	——
16	——	——	——
17	——	——	——
18	——	——	——
TOTALS	——————	—————	—————

Question #	Yes/No	Both Yes	Both No
19	——	——	——
20	——	——	——
21	——	——	——
22	——	——	——
23	——	——	——
24	——	——	——
TOTALS	———	———	———

Question #	Yes/No	Both Yes	Both No
25	——	——	——
26	——	——	——
27	——	——	——
28	——	——	——
29	——	——	——
30	——	——	——
TOTALS	———	———	———

Question #	Yes/No	Both Yes	Both No
31	___	___	___
32	___	___	___
33	___	___	___
34	___	___	___
35	___	___	___
36	___	___	___
TOTALS	_____	_____	_____

Question #	Yes/No	Both Yes	Both No
37	___	___	___
38	___	___	___
39	___	___	___
40	___	___	___
41	___	___	___
42	___	___	___
TOTALS	_____	_____	_____

Question #	Yes/No	Both Yes	Both No
43	___	___	___
44	___	___	___
45	___	___	___
46	___	___	___
47	___	___	___
48	___	___	___
TOTALS	_____	_____	_____

Question #	Yes/No	Both Yes	Both No
49	___	___	___
50	___	___	___
51	___	___	___
52	___	___	___
53	___	___	___
54	___	___	___
TOTALS	_____	_____	_____

Question #	Yes/No	Both Yes	Both No
55	——	——	——
56	——	——	——
57	——	——	——
58	——	——	——
59	——	——	——
60	——	——	——
TOTALS	————	————	————

Question #	Yes/No	Both Yes	Both No
61	——	——	——
62	——	——	——
63	——	——	——
64	——	——	——
65	——	——	——
66	——	——	——
TOTALS	————	————	————

Question #	Yes/No	Both Yes	Both No
67	—	—	—
68	—	—	—
69	—	—	—
70	—	—	—
71	—	—	—
72	—	—	—
TOTALS	—	—	—

Parent/Adolescent Test Comparison—Father

Question #	Yes/No	Both Yes	Both No
1	—	—	—
2	—	—	—
3	—	—	—
4	—	—	—
5	—	—	—
6	—	—	—
TOTALS	—	—	—

Question #	Yes/No	Both Yes	Both No
7	——	——	——
8	——	——	——
9	——	——	——
10	——	——	——
11	——	——	——
12	——	——	——
TOTALS	————	————	————

Question #	Yes/No	Both Yes	Both No
13	——	——	——
14	——	——	——
15	——	——	——
16	——	——	——
17	——	——	——
18	——	——	——
TOTALS	————	————	————

Question #	Yes/No	Both Yes	Both No
19	—	—	—
20	—	—	—
21	—	—	—
22	—	—	—
23	—	—	—
24	—	—	—
TOTALS	——	——	——

Question #	Yes/No	Both Yes	Both No
25	—	—	—
26	—	—	—
27	—	—	—
28	—	—	—
29	—	—	—
30	—	—	—
TOTALS	——	——	——

Question #	Yes/No	Both Yes	Both No
31	___	___	___
32	___	___	___
33	___	___	___
34	___	___	___
35	___	___	___
36	___	___	___
TOTALS	___	___	___

Question #	Yes/No	Both Yes	Both No
37	___	___	___
38	___	___	___
39	___	___	___
40	___	___	___
41	___	___	___
42	___	___	___
TOTALS	___	___	___

Question #	Yes/No	Both Yes	Both No
43	——	——	——
44	——	——	——
45	——	——	——
46	——	——	——
47	——	——	——
48	——	——	——
TOTALS	———	———	———

Question #	Yes/No	Both Yes	Both No
49	——	——	——
50	——	——	——
51	——	——	——
52	——	——	——
53	——	——	——
54	——	——	——
TOTALS	———	———	———

Question #	Yes/No	Both Yes	Both No
55	—	—	—
56	—	—	—
57	—	—	—
58	—	—	—
59	—	—	—
60	—	—	—
TOTALS	——	——	——

Question #	Yes/No	Both Yes	Both No
61	—	—	—
62	—	—	—
63	—	—	—
64	—	—	—
65	—	—	—
66	—	—	—
TOTALS	——	——	——

Question #	Yes/No	Both Yes	Both No
67	___	___	___
68	___	___	___
69	___	___	___
70	___	___	___
71	___	___	___
72	___	___	___
TOTALS	___	___	___

Summary Scoring Sheet

Father/Adolescent ___
Mother/Adolescent ___

Number of Questions Answered

Questions	Domain	Both Yes	Both No	Yes/No	Action Required?
1 to 6	*Moderate Freedom*	___	___	___	_____
7 to 12	*Enc. Sociability*	___	___	___	_____
13 to 18	*Enc. Indep. Thinking*	___	___	___	_____
19 to 24	*Equal Treatment*	___	___	___	_____
25 to 30	*Positive Evaluation*	___	___	___	_____
31 to 36	*Sharing*	___	___	___	_____
37 to 42	*Express Affection*	___	___	___	_____
43 to 48	*Emotional Support*	___	___	___	_____
49 to 54	*Intellectual Stim.*	___		___	_____

(continued)

55 to 60	*Being Child-Centered*	___	___	___	_____
61 to 66	*Possessiveness*	___	___	___	_____
67 to 72	*Protectiveness*	___	___	___	_____

Both Yes–total is 5 or 6. For these rows, write "NONE" under the column "Action Required?"

Both No–total is 5 or 6. For these rows, write "MAJOR" under the column "Action Required?"

Yes/No–total is 5 or 6. For these rows, write "MAJOR" under the column "Action Required?" Identify the remaining rows that do not have any entry under "ACTION REQUIRED?" For those rows, enter "MINOR" under "ACTION REQUIRED?"

SAMPLE
Summary Scoring Sheet
Father/Adolescent **X**
Mother/Adolescent ___

Number of Questions Answered

Questions	Domain	Both Yes	Both No	Yes/No	Action Required?
1 to 6	*Moderate Freedom*	5	0	1	NONE
7 to 12	*Enc. Sociability*	6	0	0	NONE
13 to 18	*Enc. Indep. Thinking*	3	1	2	MINOR
19 to 24	*Equal Treatment*	2	2	2	MINOR
25 to 30	*Positive Evaluation*	0	1	5	MAJOR
31 to 36	*Sharing*	4	0	2	MINOR
37 to 42	*Express Affection*	0	5	1	MAJOR
43 to 48	*Emotional Support*	1	0	5	MAJOR
49 to 54	*Intellectual Stim.*	5	0	1	NONE
55 to 60	*Being Child-Centered*	5	0	1	NONE
61 to 66	*Possessiveness*	2	1	3	MINOR
67 to 72	*Protectiveness*	1	2	3	MINOR

Both Yes–total is 5 or 6. For these rows, write "NONE" under the column "Action Required?".

Both No–total is 5 or 6. For these rows, write "MAJOR" under the column "Action Required?"

Yes/No–total is 5 or 6. For these rows, write "MAJOR" under the column "Action Required?" Identify the remaining rows that do not have any entry under "ACTION REQUIRED?" For those rows, enter "MINOR" under "ACTION REQUIRED?"

The scoring and analysis of this example shows:

The comparison of the test answers between the father and the adolescent indicates that the adolescent is perceiving love in the following domains and that **NO ACTION** is required to improve that perception.

Moderate freedom
Encouraging Sociability
Intellectual Stimulation
Being Child-Centered

The comparison of test answers shows that the adolescent is perceiving some love in the following domains and that **some action is required** to improve that perception.

Encouraging Independent Thinking
Equal Treatmemt
Sharing
Possessiveness
Protectiveness

The comparison of test answers shows that this adolescent is NOT perceiving love in the following domains and **major action is required** to improve that perception.

Positive Evaluation
Expressing Affection
Emotional Support

CHAPTER 9

YOU <u>CAN</u> MAKE
POSITIVE CHANGES

Do your children know you love them?

You and your children have now taken the tests to determine how much love from you they are perceiving. Chances are you've discovered some problem areas. (After all, there are no perfect parents.) You may have found that what you are feeling and trying to show may be miles apart from what your children believe they are hearing and seeing. There may be many reasons for the difference. There might be things going on in their lives that block their ability to see and hear your love. Or there might be things in your life that impair your ability to show love. If the communication gap is very wide, both you and your child are trying your best, but your children may feel very little love at all.

Don't despair. Misunderstandings are common in all human relationships. The important thing is to make an honest assessment of how things stand, then take the steps necessary to improve the situation.

In keeping with the theme of this book, our belief is that constructive change in the parent-child relationship must begin with the parents. To enhance children's perception of love, our goal is to *help parents change their own behavior.*

It is probably wrong and wasteful to seek ways of changing children's perception of parent behavior by intervening directly with the children—in effect, telling them that they have misperceived the situation. This assumes that the children's perceptions are inaccurate or incomplete. While this may or may not be true, we cannot change the misperception by simply *telling* children that they have made a mistake. Children's perceptions change when the behaviors that created them change. A child's preception of love from his/her parent isn't created out of thin air. Parents have to do things over time that resulted in the child's perception. This is not to say that the parents have done the wrong things or done the right things in the wrong way. The child has a role in all of this. But it is parents who have the capability of examining their own behavior to find better ways of actually conveying love to their child.

In the past, we assumed that a child's behavior could be changed by working directly with the child. In some areas, this will work. But in the very important area of perceiving love, it won't. Thus, it is up to the parents to change their own behaviors in order to enhance their children's perception of love.

Making positive changes begins with empathy.

For the past few months, fourteen-year-old Frederick has been smoldering with resentment toward his father. The issue is clothes. Frederick secretly believes that his father is mean and purposely hurtful because his father insists that he wear pressed button-down shirts to school. Most of the other kids wear T-shirts, and they are beginning to make fun of Frederick.

Meanwhile, Frederick's father, who grew up poor, believes he is teaching his son the importance of dressing "respectably." He wants his son to present a good image, and he is proud of the fact that he can buy his son a nice wardrobe.

While Frederick's father is acting out of love, he is acting without that ingredient that makes acts of love meaningful: empathy. If he were acting with empathy, he would be able to put himself in Frederick's shoes and see that, far from making him happy, the "nice" wardrobe is making his son's life miserable.

Without the ability to empathize with our children, all of our acts of love may fall on deaf ears, or, worse, they may actually be counterproductive. If we are astute in recognizing what is going on in our child's life, we can tailor our "love behaviors" to suit his/her life among peers, in school, and with other siblings.

You see, an important element of an adult-adult relationship is the ability to tell our partners how their actions are making us happy or unhappy. Part of this is to tell each other what we expect. Actually, we find that there is most often a difference between what each of us *believes* his/her partner expects and what the partner *actually* expects.

Similarly, a child's perception of what a parent expects, compared to what the parent actually expects, can account for some problems in the perception of love. And it is certainly a worthwhile goal that children should be able to tell their parents how their actions make them feel. But such communication skills must be learned over time, and many children simply lack the language or skills necessary to adequately understand or express why their parents' actions affect them in a certain way. Children often know they don't like something but don't know why. Are adults much different? There are people who savor the taste of broccoli. There are others who can't abide its flavor or smell. If you ask for a detailed, logical explanation of why they feel as they do about the vegetable, you will probably be told, "I can't give you specifics, but I just don't like it." Describing feelings, tastes, emotions, and other intangibles is a difficult process that needs to be learned.

That's why it is critical that parents develop the ability to empathize with their children, and that they continue to work on this skill through all the difficult years of adolescence and even beyond. While related, empathy and sympathy are not the same thing. Our definitions describe having empathy for another person as being capable of knowing how they feel in a given situation. If you know how someone feels but you don't judge that feeling, you have empathy. If you judge the situation and feel badly for the individual, you have sympathy for them.

Imagine that your two-year-old son has fallen down and scraped his knee. It is bleeding and he is crying piteously. Your immediate response is to comfort him, to ease his pain. You are feeling empathy for your hurt, innocent child. Now imagine that same child is fifteen. He is moody, withdrawn. When you ask him about his day at school, he mumbles something unintelligible and goes to his room. Even though you suspect he has had a bad day, the last thing you feel is empathy. You feel annoyed, maybe even rejected. Later on, you criticize him and an argument ensues. With empathy, you might have helped him, instead of critized him, which would have avoided an argument and shown your love.

The point of this illustration is that it is relatively easy to empathize with the simple problems of very young children. Learning to empathize with the more subtle and complex problems faced by older children and adolescents is more challenging. But their perception of our love may hinge on our ability to do just that.

In fact, we can not truly love anyone unless we are able to put ourselves in their shoes, to see things from their point of view. In short, we can not love without empathy.

It may help, as a first step, to remember those long-ago days of your own childhood and adolescence. What pain and insecurity did you suffer? What self-doubt or fears did you keep hidden from your parents because you thought they wouldn't understand? What behaviors did your parents or other authority figures demonstrate that caused you to feel hurt or confused? Conversely, what did your parents do that made you feel warm and accepted? What did they say or do that helped you understand and accept their actions?

We all have the capacity to empathize with our children, because we don't have to rely solely on our imagination to do so. In a sense, we have all "been there," in that we have all been children. By remembering our own experiences and emotions, we can more clearly understand what our children are feeling. But our memories are not always accurate.

Inevitably, we filter and modify our memories without realizing it. Thus, our memories can be guides but cannot be taken too literally.

Focus your attention on your child.

Begin by placing *all* of your attention on your child. Allow everything you do to be related to what you think is going on inside your child's mind. Try to imagine how he or she feels at that moment. Your clues will come from how the child is acting. Observe body posture and facial expression. Don't place meaning on each and every thing he or she does. Consider all of it together: Does the child look happy? Sad? Comfortable? Angry? Disappointed? Puzzled? Placid?

To a considerable degree, you are trying to step into your child's shoes. What does the child face every day? What does he or she do, see, and hear; and who acts in what way toward the child?

"Match" the child.

Milton Erickson, a pioneer in being able to bypass the conscious mind and engage the subconscious, created "matching" as an effective method of reaching another person. Matching is not mimicking. It is an attempt to be in synch with someone. First, match your child's voice—its pitch, tempo, and loudness. Then attempt to match his or her posture, breathing, and gestures. Can you find a recognizable melody in the way the child is speaking? Can you respond using the same melody? Match the cadence and volume. If the child is speaking softly and slowly, then you may want to speak softly and slowly.

Observe carefully.

Is the child breathing deeply? Is the breathing shallow and rapid? If so, shallow and rapid breathing often indicates high tension and anxiety. You might want to match this breathing at first and then assume the lead and gradually slow and deepen the breathing. On the other hand, if the child is slumped in a chair or stretched out on the floor, it isn't sensible for the adult to match that posture. (Imagine a discussion where both parent and child are stretched out on chairs across the room from each other. It might appear to be a scene out of Ancient Rome, where discussions took place in reclining positions!)

To match posture while sitting, cross your legs as your child does, or tilt your head, shrug your shoulders, or just lean forward or backward.

Developing rapport by matching and pacing is a fascinating process that produces tangible results. After being matched by another person, people say that they feel the "matcher" likes them and that there is something special between them. That step into the subconscious is something special with your child and could very well enhance the perception of love. This is a difficult process. It will take practice but will be worth the effort.

"Mirror" thoughts and feelings.

When we look in a mirror, we adjust our hair and clothing so that we look how we want to look. Children—and all of us, as psychologist Carl Rogers suggested—benefit from another kind of mirror, one in which we can hear our own thoughts and feelings from outside of ourselves. Repeating back, with pauses and slight interpretations what our children say to us, gives children an opportunity to refine their thinking and feeling, and gives us an opportunity to make sure we understood what our children have said. However, feeding back only what the child has said without any additional input from the parent might be seen as an attempt to avoid expressing an opinion. There are times when a child needs help to clarify his/her thinking or communication. Feeding back what has been said would be helpful. There are other times when the communication from the child is clear. Feeding back would be a delay tactic to avoid an opinion or answer. This hardly would enhance a perception of love.

Developing Empathy

Plays, novels, films, and poetry emotionally draw us into the characters being portrayed. Carefully drawn verbal pictures of emotional and physical beauty reach inside us and allow us to experience the emotions of the author. Often, much of the emotion we feel comes from relating to the experiences of the people portrayed. Similar feelings are present in our everyday life. A mother shares the joy of her children. Friends feel good or bad for each other. The sight of a sick or injured person upsets us. A father feels elated at the success of his children. Some of us avoid certain books, plays, or television programs because they make us feel sad.

It is possible to be moved by another person's pain and experience a desire to help. However, sharing feelings *does not always* mean help is possible. You might not know what to do to help. Or, you might know what to do, but not have the capability to do it. It is also possible that the child has to work through the problem alone, in which case your help might be counterproductive. The objective here is to increase your empathy for your child and then to translate that empathy into positive changes in parenting behavior such as knowing when to try to help and when the best course of action is to do nothing.

Here are three focused sets of activities designed to help you develop empathy. The exercise is not complete without all three areas: Imagine Self; Imagine Other; Observe Other.

Imagine Self

These activities focus on how you would feel if you were subjected to a specific set of events or conditions. When you watch another person, *imagine yourself in that person's situation and try to experience how you would feel.* Remember, you are trying to imagine how you would feel in the same situation. For instance, imagine yourself as an astronaut orbiting the earth. How would you feel walking in space? Operating a boom?

Docking with another spacecraft? What are your *feelings* as you imagine that situation?

Imagine Other

These activities are more challenging because you are being asked to forget your own feelings. You are being asked to project yourself into the *other* person's shoes and imagine how *he or she feels* and what he or she sees and hears. The goal is to experience that person's reactions to a specific situation, without projecting your own feelings onto that person. Go back to the astronaut circling the earth. In lieu of examining your own feelings, imagine how your child would feel if he/she was that astronaut. Use what you know about your child's personality to guide you.

Observe Other

Earlier in this chapter, there was a brief discussion about observing a child carefully in order to build empathy. These activities extend that discussion. Observe how your child moves his/her body. Study how your child moves the arms, legs, head, and hands. Observe his or her bearing and posture. Examine *anything* the child does. Don't try to imagine how you would feel in his or her place. Don't think about how he/she feels. Just listen and observe. You must examine both verbal and nonverbal communication. You must look for consistencies in what the child is saying verbally and what his/her body language is saying nonverbally.

For example, the child verbally participates in a family discussion. But at the same time, he keeps backing his chair farther and farther away from the table. Verbally, the child appears involved. Non-verbally, he can't seem to get away fast enough. Similarly, a child who appears open to feedback or honest discussion, but who sits with her arms wrapped tightly around her body, is sending a message that she feels vulnerable and is trying to protect herself. There are other clear, observable signals which tell a great deal about what the child is feeling.

How to develop more empathy for your child

The activities suggested here should be performed with a partner. The partner may be your spouse, a close friend, or a grandparent—someone who is familiar with your child. Your partner will also learn to develop empathy for the child this way. Select a convenient time and place to do Imagine Self and Imagine Other activities. The child *should not* be present while you explore your own feelings.

You and your partner should perform the Observe Other activity separately. Over the course of a week, each of you should record your answers to the questions in the section that follows. At the end of the week, schedule some private time so that the two of you can compare notes. Again, the child *should not* be present.

Imagine Self

1. Select only those situations to discuss that are appropriate for your child's age and interests. To help, we have clustered the activities by age.

2. You may create and add other situations to discuss. Please write down any new situations so that your partner and you are clear about which situation you are discussing.

*Allow yourself to be a child again, experiencing these situations as yourself. How would **you feel if**...*

Preteens
A. Your parents received a failing warning notice from your school.
B. You received an athletic award.
C. Your parents scolded you for "not acting your age" at a recent neighborhood party.
D. Your parents grounded you for not cleaning your room.
E. You learned that one of your classmates had committed suicide.

Teens
F. You dented a fender while driving the family car (without permission).
G. You dented a fender while driving the family car (with permission).
H. You broke up with your boyfriend or girlfriend.
I. You received a promotion at work.
J. You saw one of your friends using marijuana.
K. You saw one of your friends get drunk.
L. You saw one of your friends using hard drugs.
M. You learned that one of your friends was pregnant.
N. You learned that one of your close friends committed suicide.

Imagine Other

1. Select only those situations to discuss that are appropriate for your child's age and interests. To help, we have clustered the activities by age.

2. You may create and add other situations to discuss. Please write down any new situations so that your partner and you are clear about which situation you are discussing.

*Set aside your own experiences, feelings, and attitudes. Project your-self into your child's mind and emotions to describe how you think your **son/daughter would feel if** . . .*

PreTeens

  A. His/her parents received a failing warning notice from school.

  B. He/she received an athletic award.

  C. His/her parents scolded him/her for "not acting his/her age" at a neighborhood party.

  D. His/her parents grounded him/her for not cleaning his/her room.

  E. He/she learned that one of his/her classmates had committed suicide.

Teens

  F. He/she dented a fender while driving the family car (without permission).

  G. He/she dented a fender while driving the family car (with permission).

  H. He/she broke up with his/her boyfriend or girlfriend.

  I. He/she received a promotion at work.

  J. He/she saw one of his/her friends using marijuana.

  K. He/she saw one of his/her friends get drunk.

  L. He/she saw one of his/her friends using hard drugs.

  M. He/she learned that one of his/her friends was pregnant.

  N. He/she learned that one of his/her close friends committed suicide.

Observe Other

1. Select only those situations to discuss that are appropriate for your child's age and interests. To help, we have clustered the activities by age.

2. You may create and add other situations to discuss. Please write down any new situations so that your partner and you are clear about which situation you are discussing. _Try as best as you are able to describe the language and words your child used. Describe your sense of what the child was saying and was not saying. Describe body language, behavior, emotions, and interactions with others that give you a sense of what the child was feeling and not saying. Specifically, how did your son/daughter act when . . ._

PreTeens

A. His/her parents received a failing warning notice from school.
B. He/she received an athletic award.
C. His/her parents scolded him/her for "not acting his/her age" at a neighborhood party.
D. His/her parents grounded him/her for not cleaning his/her room.
E. He/she learned that one of his/her classmates had committed suicide.

Teens

F. He/she dented a fender while driving the family car (without permission).
G. He/she dented a fender while driving the family car (with permission).
H. He/she broke up with his/her boyfriend or girlfriend.
I. He/she received a promotion at work.
J. He/she saw one of his/her friends using marijuana.
K. He/she saw one of his/her friends get drunk.
L. He/she saw one of his/her friends using hard drugs.
M. He/she learned that one of his/her friends was pregnant.
N. He/she learned that one of his/her close friends committed suicide.

Doing these exercises will give you a "running start" in understanding your child's feelings in many different situations. You will be surprised to discover how many verbal and non-verbal cues you miss the first few times you do these exercises. Your partner's observations will help you improve over time. The exercises are the first step, but you'll need to boost your awareness to a higher level periodically. At about six month intervals, we suggest that you do at least some of the exercises here.

Empathy is not permissiveness.

Developing empathy for your children is a crucial tool in enhancing their perception of love from you. But it is important to recognize that empathy is not an excuse for allowing children to do anything they choose at any time simply because you, as the parent, know how they feel. Often people who attempt to convince you to do something *they* want you to do will work at having you empathize with them. Have you noticed that many automobile salespeople have photographs of their children prominently displayed in their sales offices? Have you also noticed that much of their conversation includes their attempts to win sales contests, their children's needs, or how hard they work to earn a living? They are attempting to get you to empathize with them—to make you like them and therefore be more susceptible to their attempts at persuasion.

The research evidence is very strong that for children, one important part of perceiving love is *seeing love with control.* Children need and desire some boundaries in their lives. Total freedom is often threatening and frightening to a child. It is possible to know what is happening in your children's lives and to feel their emotions and *still* be the parent responsible for setting boundaries.

An excellent guide for setting boundaries is the notion of a "comfort zone." Think of a furnace's thermostat; nearly everyone in the house would be comfortable between 65°F and 75°F. Similarly, each household must establish its own comfort zone in which chores are completed; curfews are met; and other responsibilities are fulfilled. There is plenty of freedom—*within that zone.*

Expectations

In its simplest form, an expectation is one person's prediction of what another person will do. Sometimes the expectation is very clear. However, expectations vary based on who perceives them. Two parents might say that they believe their children grew up to be the kinds of people they can be proud of. However, not many people see their children's behavior the same way the parents do—including the children themselves. Some of it is wishful thinking, some of it is poor observation, and some of it is real.

When parents communicate an expectation to their children—deliberately or not—children try to live up to that expectation *as they perceive it.* Unfortunately, what they perceive may cause them to reach for the heights or descend to the depths in response to exactly the same information.

We can't classify expectations as being either good or bad. Those which seem to be good might easily become problems if carried to extremes. A parent might want too much. And a child may feel that he/she must meet all expectations—including the unreasonable ones.

The Roots of Expectations

Parents' expectations of their children develop from two major sources. Parents learn what to expect of their children based on what they know about them. Parents also develop expectations of children based on what they learn by listening to and observing family, community, peers, television, and other sources, and then applying them to their own children. Because this is not firsthand knowledge, it suffers from exaggeration, misperception, and a lack of reality. Parents need to use their own experiences and knowledge of *their* children. They can also merge their information with society's ideals.

Living Up to Expectations

It is quite natural for parents to have expectations of their children. It is also quite natural for the parent to convey these expectations in words and behavior to the child. But in order for a parent's expectations to have an impact on the child's behavior, three conditions need to be present.

First, the child must believe that he/she can do what the expectation requires. The child needs to believe that he/she has the physical, intellectual, social, emotional, and moral ability to do what is expected. *If the child doesn't believe that he can do it, he won't.* Thus for a child to believe that he can meet the expectation, he needs to have the proper "equipment."

Second, the child needs to believe that if she does what is expected by the parent, positive things will follow. Simply, "If I do what you expect of me, can I be sure that what you say will happen, will happen?" It is easy to make promises to a child to get them to do what you want and expect. Unfortunately, many of the promises made do not lead to predictable results. Some examples are:

"Do your homework and you'll be at the top of your class."

"Say your prayers every night and only good things will happen to you."

"Eat all your vegetables and you will be the strongest child in your class."

These results are hardly predictable, even if the child could live up to your expectations.

Third, the child must truly want the same thing the parent does. The value of meeting an expectation can only be measured from the view of the child. If the child doesn't think meeting the expectation is worthwhile, he won't do it.

In studies to determine why female students began to achieve poorly in math and science when entering high school, a surprising result was that female students believed that if they achieved in math and science, they would not do as well socially. They believed that boys did not like girls who achieved academically. Thus, the expectation from parents to do well in math and science was not a personally desired outcome. Of course, these girls had the capability. If they applied themselves to math and science, the result would be academic achievement. The problem was that they did not desire the result.

Unrealistic expectations may lead to disappointment for the parent and the child, and disappointment is found at the root of anger. Thus, to avoid anger, it is necessary to realign your expectations with the ability of your children to meet them.

Realigning Expectations

Before trying this approach with your children, we suggest that two adults in a life partnership try it with each other. Agree upon an area of expectation which you want to examine. Examples include: finances, emotional support, work habits, dress, health practices, and preferences in food, entertainment, and travel. The list might include almost any aspect of the relationship.

Each adult should answer the following question on a separate sheet of paper.

1. What do I expect of you (financially, emotionally, in work habits, etc.)?

Using additional paper, each adult should answer a second question.

2. What do I believe you expect of me (on the same issue as the first question)?

When complete, exchange the answers to Question 1. Now each partner has the answers to what the other person actually expects of him/her and his/her _own_ answer to What he/she believes the other person expects. The comparisons can now be made between real and imagined expectations.

In our experience, this exercise and the resulting dialogue opens eyes. Much of the time, an individual is far too hard on him or herself. The adults find themselves attempting to meet an imagined expectation—which can be more difficult to achieve than the real expectation. Joint discussion and clarification of what is truly expected will reduce frustration and anger in the relationship.

With the experience gained by examining mutual expectations with your partner, now attempt a similar exercise with your adolescent. As before, agree on a subject area and use the two questions to start the discussion. The results will be worthwhile.

It will be more difficult to attempt this exercise with the pre-adolescent unless the subject area is very specific and understandable to the child. Topics might include doing chores around the house, personal cleanliness, picking up after oneself, and relationships with other siblings. Save doing the exercise with the pre-adolescent for last. Start with your partner, move on to an adolescent, then attempt the exercise with younger children.

People need to understand what is expected of them. In order for them to meet expectations held by others, those expectations must be realistic and based on the individual's capability, the predictability of the result and, finally, the value that the individual finds in meeting the expectation. This is true of both adults and children.

CHAPTER 10

THE CREDIBILITY FACTOR

So far in our discussion of improving parent-child relationships, we have focused on developing empathy with the child. Some of you may be wondering if the child shouldn't learn to feel a little empathy toward the parents, as well. After all, parenting is one of life's most challenging jobs!

Our response is that children do learn empathy toward their parents, albeit slowly, if the parents are willing to share their own feelings and experiences—to reveal themselves as fellow human beings. But in the self-focused world of childhood and adolescence, most youngsters lack the maturity to sustain feelings of empathy with their parents.

A more realistic goal—and one that will go far toward helping you make the changes needed to improve your children's perception of love—is for your children to see you as *credible.*

Being credible means being believable.

To believe what you say or do, your child has to trust you. But to trust you, the child has to believe you. Credibility and trust are intertwined. Enhancing one will enhance the other. Some facts about credibility and trust:

• *You are credible if your child believes you know what you are talking about and that you will not profit personally by misleading him or her.* There are areas of knowledge in which your children generally accept you as expert. As they grow up, the children will often turn to you, the parent, for guidance and advice in the real, tangible areas of life such as finances, education, nutrition, and housing. Other than observing what you do, most children generally do not turn to parents for advice where others are the experts—such as which boy likes which girl at school. They acquire peer-oriented knowledge from their peer group—individuals they believe to be experts in their growing social world.

• *You are credible if your child sees you as being enthusiastic, dynamic, safe, kind, congenial, friendly, agreeable, pleasant, gentle, unselfish, just, forgiving, fair, hospitable, warm, cheerful, ethical, calm, patient, and capable of admitting when you don't know something.* Unfortunately, no parent is capable of being all these things to a child all of the time. At best, when we try to establish trust, we hope that our child has recognized many of these positive qualities in us.

• *You are more credible if you draw upon information and opinions of authorities who already have credibility.* If you plan to talk with your children about drug abuse, be aware that school drug-counselors are seen as knowing a lot about drugs and a lot about people. Physicians, pharmacists, and chemists are seen as knowing much about drugs but little about the people who use them. Clergy are seen as knowing much about people but little about drugs.

In this sense, children are quite logical in their approach. If you needed information about camping, to whom would you turn? Obviously, to a camper. If you wanted career information about teaching, you would turn to someone who was connected to the profession. There's nothing startling here.

• *You are credible if your child holds you in high esteem.* But remember that the level of esteem varies with the subject and situation, so don't automatically assume anything.

Three favorite statements parents often make when they try to add to their credibility:

"Trust me. I've taken care of you until now, and I know what's best for you."

"Trust me. As your father (mother), I have only your best interests at heart."

"Fathers have always had the final say about things like this— and I AM YOUR FATHER."

The assumption made is that credibility is built into the role as "the parent." To some degree, it is. When children are quite young, parents are the source of almost all rewards— emotional and physical. As children mature, other adults and members of the peer group become sources for rewards, as well. When parents lose the ability to reinforce their wishes by using rewards, or repeatedly turn aside children's requests for information (for example, information about sex), parents' inherent credibility wanes. Interestingly, the credibility regains strength as the children become adults and have children of their own. Mature children have been known to comment, "It is amazing how much more my parents knew as I grew older."

• *To remain credible, the parent cannot embellish facts or use biased, inaccurate information.* Also, if the child's own experience doesn't match with the story the parent tells, credibility will suffer. Parents who vehemently oppose the marriage of their child to a person of another religion often use a rationale that such couples divorce more frequently. They also report that the reasons for divorce among interfaith couples are said to be because of religious and cultural differences. The evidence is contradictory. Interfaith married couples divorce no more frequently than other similar age couples, and do so for the same reasons as couples who share the same religious background. Parent credibility will be reduced if you use the fear of more frequent divorce as information to deter intermarriage.

• *Credibility suffers when a parent who is expert in an area allows his or her personal bias to tarnish the information offered.* As examples, consider the health professional who zealously tells an adolescent that smoking a marijuana cigarette will hopelessly addict him permanently. The parent should know this isn't true, and it's likely the child knows it, too.

• *Credibility suffers when a parent or authority appears out of touch with the children's daily social circumstances.* As a drug-prevention activity, a senior high school we know of invited a local narcotics squad police officer to address the student body. During the presentation, the officer distributed three marijuana cigarettes to be examined by the students. The intent was to show "innocent" adolescents what the marijuana looked like. At the end of the lecture, the police officer received the three marijuana cigarettes he had distributed and an additional one—a present from the student body.

• *The parent who uses examples of experiences (either the parent's or those of other people) to enhance credibility should use positive experiences.* Overly negative information arouses fear; fear reduces the ability to absorb information; the net result is reduced credibility. It is far better to use a Horatio Alger-type success story to illustrate your point than to use a terrible tale of woe designed to frighten. The current evaluation evidence on programs presented by prison inmates designed to frighten high-school students into "staying out of trouble" indicates limited short-term success. A positive role model can have a more dramatic long-term impact. There is evidence that negative tales result in the child's belief that if the storyteller could overcome the problem, so might the child. That may or may not be true.

In one community in which we worked with parents, it emerged that before training, parents had a standard conversation with their children about sex, drugs, or other topics like HIV and other serious illnesses. It went like this:

CHILD: Everyone says our neighbor died of AIDS. What is AIDS? (Child request for information.)
PARENT: You can get AIDS from sex. Don't have sex or you'll die. (Parent invokes negative consequences.)
CHILD: I won't. (Child reassures parent and conversation stops.)
    The child still had the fact about the neighbor and a new

set of attitudes—HIV/AIDS is something difficult to talk about.

Contrast the following conversation where the parent "heard" the underlying concerns of the child.

CHILD: What is AIDS?

PARENT: It is the last stage of an illness caused by a particular virus called the Human Immunodeficiency Virus or HIV.

CHILD: How do you get it? Everyone says our neighbor had it.

PARENT: It is actually hard to catch. You get it from infected blood or other body fluids getting into your body and past your body's defenses. Most people get it from sex or sharing syringes for injections.

CHILD: You mean I probably don't have it. I played with the neighbor's cat. It's okay that I liked my neighbor?

The child in this conversation had his unspoken question answered and his fears soothed. In the process, his parent's credibility increased.

As we have said, credibility and trust are vital to children's perception of love. Building and maintaining credibility requires that parents be aware of their own behavior, and that they be willing to change behaviors that have damaged their credibility.

Making changes requires time and patience—and consistent effort. There is much to do. There is much to do again. The key is to *continue* doing and redoing.

CHAPTER 11

THE TRUST FACTOR

Trust helps relationships flourish.

A mother and her fifteen-year-old daughter returned from a day of shopping. As they entered the front door, it was evident that something was wrong. Tension and anger filled the air. Their voices were increasing in volume, and the dispute was getting more intense.

The day had started as a long-awaited mother-daughter shopping expedition for summer clothes. All went well until they reached the swimwear department of the store. The dispute centered on the amount of skin displayed when the daughter wore certain swimsuits. The mother refused to allow the purchase of swimsuits that revealed more than she thought was "decent." With the resultant stalemate and the ensuing argument, the pair returned home.

As the dispute continued, the daughter insisted that her friends were allowed to wear revealing swimsuits that were as skimpy or skimpier than the one she wanted. The mother doubted that the parents she knew would allow their daughters to wear such swimsuits. As the accusations and complaints rocketed back and forth, they broadened to include every hurt and problem experienced by either the mother or daughter at the hands of the other during the past several years. Finally the frustrated mother exclaimed, "Why can't we discuss this like two normal people?"

The daughter's immediate response was, "Because I am afraid to trust you." Deeply hurt and with tears in her eyes, the mother turned and left the room.

How do we earn our children's trust?

Nothing weakens a relationship more quickly than a loss of trust. Indeed, trust is a necessary ingredient in any healthy relationship. Without trust, love can not flourish.

Children's perception of trust changes as they mature. Very young children seem to relate trust to physical strength and capability. They might reason, "If I give him my toy, he won't break it. He isn't strong enough." From about five to seven years of age, children recognize that intention and motivation are involved along with capability. They believe that they can trust friends who will do whatever they tell them to do.

As children mature into adolescence, their understanding of trust deepens. They see it as a balance of doing things for each other. It becomes a significant part of relationships, where individuals provide support or clarification for each other's intimate and personal concerns. Friends (and loving parents) can be relied on to tell the truth in a genuine and nonhurtful way. Friends can be relied upon not to use your intimate concerns against you.

How does trust develop? It grows as a result of mutual prudent risk taking. Learning to have interpersonal trust starts with taking a risk and trusting another person with knowledge of your intimate and personal concerns. Each time an individual takes a risk by sharing intimate concerns with another person, and is rewarded with trustworthiness, two things occur. First, the confidant feels encouraged to take a risk in return. Second, the individual who took the initial risk is now more confident of taking a risk again. Mutual risk-taking leads to increased levels of trust.

There are many levels of trust. Trust can be defined as *ex pecting that the words or promises of another person are reliable.* But the daughter's comment "I am afraid to trust you" is difficult to comprehend. Since birth, this girl trusted her mother to nurture her, to provide food, clothing, emotional support, companionship, and money. And now she says that she is afraid to trust her mother. Afraid to trust her about *what?*

Somehow, this teenage girl believes that her mother has violated or will violate her daughter's interpersonal trust. Considering her comment, it is likely that the trust violation has not yet occurred. There is hope that trust can be restored or maintained. We know that future trust will be related to parent consistency, predictability, and how important the specific action or information is to the child.

For example, how would you fare in an environment where your boss praises you today for generating new ideas and berates you tomorrow for wasting his/her time with all this foolishness? Or consider the problem of growing up in a home where your parent is caring and loving today, distant and uncaring tomorrow, and caring and loving again the following day. The children of alcoholic parents try to learn to cope with a relationship in which parent behavior or reactions are unpredictable. Thus, two necessary ingredients in building and maintaining a trust relationship is to be consistent in what you do and why you do it. This will lead to your behavior being completely predictable—perhaps not exciting, but far more trustworthy.

The third ingredient is how important the situation is to the person who has to have the trust. Asking for directions is not a high-risk situation. The downside risk is either being embarrassed at having to ask or—at worst—getting lost. Trusting someone to teach you how to ride a bicycle is a bit more risky. If they are not careful, you might fall and be hurt. Selecting an instructor to teach you swimming or mountain climbing is riskier still. As we increase the chance of being hurt physically or being "betrayed interpersonally," trust becomes more difficult to develop and maintain.

In this situation in which the daughter said that she couldn't trust her mother, we believe that there is another fear at work. We suspect that the mother *lacks credibility* with her daughter in her actions about what is appropriate clothing. The daughter believes that her mother doesn't know enough about her need to conform to the dress norms of her peer group. She also believes that her friends' parents know a lot more about peer-group pressures than her mother. To have prevented the dispute, or to start to resolve it now, this mother needs to deal with her credibility.

The point has been made frequently here that to gain trust from someone, you have to give trust. Perhaps with credibility in the eyes of her daughter, the mother might have established standards for buying appropriate clothing and then trusted her daughter to live up to those standards. The standards would have been mutually established, giving the mother credibility and her daughter the chance to learn to trust her judgment. The girl might have trusted her mother to understand her need to conform to her peer group without resorting to fanciful, inaccurate statements regarding the parents of her peers. In turn, the daughter would have become more credible to her mother. Conscious, focused efforts to enhance credibility and trust might have provided an answer to the mother's question: "Why can't we discuss this like two normal people?"

When trust is damaged or lost, there is a danger that the problem can spiral out of control. It won't get better by itself. While time might be an excellent healer in some cases, the passage of time here most often hurts rather than helps restore lost trust.

The first and most important step is to let the child know that while the two of you disagree on one issue, you have not stopped loving him/her. First, allow the heat of the anger to cool in each of you—at least until you acknowledge each other's presence and can act in a civil way toward each other. Then, when you are alone, tell him/her that you regret the disagreement and that you still love him/her. There's no doubt that this is a risk. You risk rejection from your child and a feeling of humiliation. However, this is the risk necessary to re-establish trust.

The child may reject your overture. If so, wait a few days

and try again. The child might respond with only a quizzical look and a grunt. You might then say, "I still disagree with what you want, but I know there are many things that we agree on." Try to begin a dialogue about something positive—something you *can* agree on.

We believe that at some point, the child will also begin to take a risk toward rebuilding trust. He/she knows that the split is not forever. This is not to imply that the child won't test you by reopening the discussion to try to win his/her way. But the door will be open to discussion—a crucial time to show love and have the child perceive it.

CHAPTER 12

BUT MY CHILD'S SO ANGRY!

Some parent-child relationships have become so seriously damaged that the child perceives little love from the parent. The child may reject the parent's efforts at rebuilding the relationship, and may even seem to take a kind of perverse pleasure in trying to tear it further apart. The child is angry. If we look just below the anger, we will find disappointment. The child is disappointed at something the parent has or has not done. Often, not feeling or perceiving love from a parent can result in powerful anger—powerful enough to destroy a relationship.

Such a seriously damaged relationship will no doubt benefit from the intervention of a competent psychologist who specializes in family therapy. In these cases it is imperative that the therapist build a trusting relationship with the child so that the child will feel secure enough to open up and reveal his or her true feelings. Sticking a bandage of improved behavior on these relationships won't do much good if the underlying issues are allowed to fester unaddressed.

On the other hand, there are steps that parents can take to start improving the strained relationship—whether or not the situation is critical enough to call in a psychological professional.

Make a molehill out of a mountain.

People usually tell us to deal with "the bigger picture" when we try to solve problems. The implication is that we get caught up in smaller day-to-day problems that block our ability to try to do something about larger, more significant problems. Conventional wisdom has suggested that we ignore the small problems in order to deal with larger ones. This assumption has recently been called into question. New research indicates that we might be better off dealing with smaller problems and letting the bigger ones take care of themselves.

In talking with the owners-managers of some small and growing businesses, we learned that most of them had suffered mild anxiety attacks when thinking of the long-term future. They awoke from sleep worrying about problems that might surface six months to a year later.

They said that when they focused on the problems they would face during the next several weeks and let the longer-term problems take care of themselves, things worked out better. They were aware of the long-term problems, and of the options for solving them, but they did little about them immediately. The available energy and effort went into solving the near-term, smaller-scope problems.

A similar pattern evolves in dealing with difficult and demanding relationships. (And, for many adults, their children represent difficult and demanding relationships—albeit with great rewards, but still demanding and difficult.) Adults can become highly agitated and annoyed by children's, particularly adolescents', behavior. The rapid increase in agitation and emotional arousal often clouds parental thought processes. With the high state of emotional arousal, parents may lose much of their ability to cope with their children's behavior. Simply, the more angry you become, the more likely it is that your emotions will rule the situation rather than your intelligence.

For example, a major focus in substance-abuse prevention

efforts today advises parents to talk to their children about drugs. However, parents are cautioned *not to discuss* drugs with their children when the parents are angry. In particular, the parents are told that if they discover drugs or drug paraphernalia among their children's things, "calm down and think of what you will say. Decide what you need to accomplish and do it calmly." Somehow, we seem to believe that if a child isn't listening to what we say, he/she will hear us better if we yell and scream. There is no correlation between increased volume of a parent's voice and the level of understanding and acceptance by the child. If anything, the reverse is probably true.

We have learned that people are good problem solvers when they believe that the problem to be solved isn't very important in their lives. This might explain why it appears easier to solve another person's problems rather than our own. When the problem is approached as if "it's not as difficult as all that," we suffer far less anxiety and arousal. We need to find ways to reduce problems into smaller and less intense units. Then, we can usually focus more easily and solve them quickly.

Take small steps.

Obviously, changing a situation where your child does not perceive love from you is not an easy thing to do. It is not likely that you deliberately avoid showing love, or that the child just doesn't want to recognize it. First you have to understand what you did or failed to do. Then estimate what you think you can do about the situation. Then act, and finally evaluate the results of your actions.

Rarely do we find that a child perceives no love at all, or that the parent believes he or she is showing love in all areas and the child doesn't see any of it. In lieu of believing the situation is totally out of control, it is possible to find those areas where the relationship is good and love is perceived. Then, identify one—and only one—area where a problem in perception of love exists. Work on that single area rather than the entire relationship. Start with one of the "minor" problems as identified in the tests you took, rather than on a "major" one.

Simply, instead of looking for a big win over the big problem, seek a smaller win over a smaller problem.

For example, if you were to tell your teenager that you don't approve of *all* his friends, you create a large problem for him. Assuming he agrees with you about the friends, would he be able to replace all of them at the same time? You might help him find new places to meet some new friends while he tries to replace those that both of you find unacceptable.

Put things in perspective.

Several years ago, we participated in an exercise program at a local hospital. The activities were supervised at the time by a registered nurse, who was in the third trimester of pregnancy. One day she described a phone conversation with her husband, who was on a business trip. He had mentioned sharing a glass of wine over dinner with a female colleague, unwittingly lighting the fuse of his wife's anger at the "bimbo." His wife would not consume any alcoholic beverages during her pregnancy and missed the occasional glass of wine she once enjoyed with a meal. She was also unhappy with the way her appearance had changed during her pregnancy. Her husband was due to return the following day, and the nurse was very, very angry. In great detail, she described "getting even with her husband."

One of us asked her if she was going to divorce her husband over this incident. She said, "Of course not." We then asked, "Are you planning any other drastic action to punish him?" She replied, "No."

The next question was, "When will you stop being angry? Since you are not considering divorce or other drastic action, you obviously expect to stop being angry at some point in time. When will that be?"

She thought for a moment or two and answered, "Two days after he gets home."

We let it go at that.

About fifteen minutes later, she approached us and asked in a much calmer tone, "How did you do that?"

"Do what?"

She said, "I'm not angry at my husband anymore. How come?"

We replied that we hadn't done anything. All we did was ask her a question or two. She did the rest.

What we had done was to bring her awareness that she wouldn't be *permanently* angry into her conscious mind. She already knew that she wouldn't be permanently angry in her subconscious. Once the conscious awareness was there, her anger dissipated.

A similar approach could help with an annoyed, angry, or suspicious child. First, acknowledge the child's mood. Tell the child that you know he or she is angry or annoyed at you. If you know the reason for the anger, acknowledge the reason— neither agreeing nor disagreeing that the reason is valid. Using a soft voice, ask what the slightly distant future holds for both of you and when he or she will be ready to "be friends" with you again.

You need to gauge your questions to be relevant for the age and maturity of the child. Children without an appreciation or understanding of time cannot be asked whether they will "always" be angry or if they will "run away from home." The goal is to make the child aware that at some time in the future, he/she will no longer be angry. If this can be accomplished, the child's current anger or annoyance will dissipate.

Sometimes, a child won't want to let go of his/her anger. It's as if this episode gave rise to the anger that had been building for some time. And the anger has acted as a stimulant—allowing the child to say and do things that he/she would not have done before. Anger can significantly reduce one's inhibitions, allowing an individual to do some uncharacteristic things. Often, the child learns some of these responses to anger from the parent. If you yell, scream, throw objects, strike out against walls, sulk, or glare when you're mad, you teach youngsters to do the same. Giving vent in these ways is a new experience for the child—one that is stimulating, exciting, and perceived as dangerous. But are you happy to see your child mirror angry, immature, and destructive behavior?

CHAPTER 13

DEALING WITH TEENAGERS— A JOINT EFFORT

A startling change occurs when a child becomes an adolescent. Bizarre, often unpredictable swings in mood from one extreme to another characterize many emerging adolescents. It is not unusual for dislikes to turn into cravings and back to dislikes again in a very short time. Adultlike behavior can be replaced by childlike behavior before parents have time to react. Thought becomes increasingly abstract and more comprehensive. Adolescents become capable of thinking about *why* they're thinking about something. They start to think about reality rather than dealing with reality itself. They develop a preoccupation with understanding their own behavior, motivation, perceptions, successes, and failures. And they are even more capable of comprehending the abstractions of love.

As they examine the reasons for success or failure, some adolescents may blame their environment for failure and take personal credit for success. Thus, they believe they succeed because they are good at what they do. They believe they fail because their parents, their schools, and their communities have failed them in not providing the skills nor the environment necessary to succeed. The evidence is that these adolescents are not able to learn very much about how to succeed in the future. Conversely, those adolescents who blame themselves for failure and credit their environments for success are in a position to benefit from feedback about succeeding. If one knows that he/she didn't do enough of the right things to succeed, the opportunity is there to learn.

Those of you who have adolescent children are in a unique and wonderful position to make positive changes in your relationship with your child. The testing and data analyses have pinpointed the problem areas in your adolescent's perception of love from you. You have been able to focus on those domains in need of major and minor change, and which can be left alone. You have been able to compare your *understanding* of what your adolescent perceives with his or her actual perceptions.

Remember, the five factors that determine whether and how adolescents perceive love from their parents are:

- **What** parents do.
- **Why** parents do it (as seen by the adolescent).
- **When** parents do it.
- **Which** other options for actions exist.
- **Who** benefits by what was done.

Thus, the plans we make for change in the perception of love must include methods of dealing with these five factors. But now, the plans for change and the way we carry out those plans are not only in the hands of the parents. The adolescent has a significant role, and as someone who understands the abstraction of love, he/she must be consulted about what has to be changed and how to change it. Parents cannot mandate the changes alone.

Talking about love with your teen requires careful preparation.

Before you open a serious discussion with your adolescent about changing your behavior, it would probably be helpful to create an action plan as follows:

1. Look at the summary scoring form and identify those domains which require action for improvement. Select one of the major or minor action domains. Schedule a time for the discussion that is mutually convenient for both of you, and be sure that you both have sufficient time to discuss the area thoroughly.

2. Prepare in advance for the meeting or discussion with the teenager. You could bring some brief notes to jog your memory, but don't use a prepared script outlining what you will say.

3. Be prepared to share and to listen. It needs to be said again: Be prepared to *share* and to *listen*. Try not to judge what your adolescent says. Use what you have learned about communication, empathy, matching, and mirroring to listen effectively.

4. Hold the discussion in private—just you and your adolescent. Often at home, we lack the available private space to hold a private conversation. Talking while "taking a walk" is private. Sitting together in a park also provides privacy. Without privacy, the conversation and discussion will be limited.

5. Allow enough time to talk through at least one of the domains you select for examination and change. Frequently examining your watch during the conversation tells the adolescent that you are impatient, that time is running out, i.e. "Let's get on with it." This is hardly the way to convey love and caring to your adolescent. Allowing enough time is not just a function of the minutes available for the dialogue. It also conveys that this conversation is among the most important things that you have to do.

6. Before starting the dialogue about the perception of love, tell the teenager what this is all about. If you wish, tell the adolescent about reading *Do Your Kids Know You Love Them?* Tell your child how important you believe the perception of love is to both of you. Talk about taking the tests and how this discussion stems from the

comparison of both tests. And, finally, tell the adolescent what you hope will come from the discussion. You might ask the adolescent what he or she would like to see come from the discussion. **Be honest. Be sincere. And above all else, listen, listen, listen.**

7. Have the discussion with your adolescent. When you've started to make the changes both of you agreed upon, repeat the process for a second action you need to take.

8. Select a date about three months from now. On or about that date, repeat the tests and analyses to measure any progress. It has been our experience that by the time parents and adolescents have met and discussed these needs two or three times, ways of enhancing the perception of love will be part of their lives. The growth will continue for as long as you wish. It's up to your adolescent and you to decide.

CHAPTER 14

BUILDING THE PERCEPTION
OF LOVE

Most parents understand intuitively the importance of love in a child's life. As we have stated throughout this book, feeling loved can have a positive, lasting impact on children's social, physical, and psychological well-being. Conversely, feeling unloved has been shown to correlate with drug and alcohol abuse, poor school performance, physical ailments, and certain antisocial behaviors.

Unfortunately, while most parents do in fact love their children, many of those children do not *perceive* that love. This is because between parents and children, as in all human relationships, a deep gulf between reality and perception can exist.

As we have said, what parents believe they are showing and what their children are perceiving may be two very different things.

An example of this is a fourteen-year-old girl we encountered who was engaging in sexually promiscuous behavior. Her parents were horrified when they found out. They loved her very much, took her to church each Sunday to instill values, and worked hard to provide many of the material goods they had lacked in their own youths. In their minds, they had done everything right. But when this child was asked about her parents' feelings about her, she said in a bleak voice, "Oh, they care about me. As long as it doesn't interfere with their own lives." Try as they might, her parents could not understand her perception.

Another child, whose parents also professed to love him, remarked that he didn't like to go home because home was where he felt most lonely. And that feeling persisted even when his parents were at home *with* him.

These two examples illustrate our point that children whose parents believe they are loving sometimes feel unloved—with devastating consequences.

Our larger point, however—and the crux of this book—is that in order for a child's perception to change, his/her parents must change the way they show love—including what they do, why they do it, when it is done, which option they choose, and who benefits from it.

When dealing with a child who does not accurately comprehend a parent's feelings, many parents or mental health professionals are tempted to "work with the child" in order to correct the misperception, assuming that the child is somehow confused and that the work to be done should focus on "fixing" the confusion.

We place the focus where we feel it more properly belongs—on the parent. For it is the *parent's* behaviors, words, and attitudes that have created the child's misperception that he/she is not loved. And it is only by changing those behaviors, words, and attitudes that a perception of love can be created.

Perceiving care from others

A school in one of the poorest areas of a large city in the northeastern United States was surrounded by a large railway yard, a factory, and a brothel. At the time this research was done, about a third of the children were African Americans; the balance were Caucasian. Boys and girls had their own entrances to the school, and used separate basements and play areas. Children moved from place to place in a formal line with the girls in front and the boys behind. The children were often unruly, fighting with each other, and were punished for it—including being strapped.

Teachers only reluctantly accepted assignments to this school. As soon as the opportunity became available, they moved on. Principals were hired and assigned but also moved on after a brief tenure. However, a solid core of experienced teachers continued to teach at this school. There were three first-grade teachers—Ms. Allen, Ms. Baker, and Ms. Call. Researchers located thirty males and thirty females who had been first-grade students at this school and were now adults, twenty-five years later. During interviews, these former students were asked to evaluate the effectiveness of their former first-grade teachers, to grade their efforts, and to make comments about their overall performance.

The result was remarkable. The achievements of individuals who had been assigned to Ms. Allen was far higher than those assigned to Ms. Baker or Ms. Call. High status jobs—such as professor, physician, accountant—had been achieved by about sixty-seven percent of her students compared to less than half by students who had the other teachers. The students involved had been taught by these teachers over an eleven-year period. Interestingly, almost seventy-five percent of the students reported that Ms. Allen had been their teacher—which was later discovered to be untrue. Remembering her warmth and concern, these students began to believe that they had been taught by Ms. Allen.

Ms. Allen was in the final stages of a terminal illness at the time of this study and could not be interviewed. Not only did she have a good reputation as a teacher, but she was still remembered by the interviewed students twenty-five years after they had been her students. Compared to other first-grade teachers, seventy-one percent rated her efforts as excellent and seventy-five percent also rated her performance as excellent. The other teachers were rated "excellent" by thirty percent and "as motivated" by twenty-five percent.

It was said of Ms. Allen's teaching ability that "it did not matter what background or abilities the beginning pupil had; there was no way that the pupil was not going to read by the end of first grade." She left her pupils with a profound impression of the importance of schooling and perseverance. If a child forgot his lunch, she would give him some of her own, and often stayed after hours to help children with their work. When asked how Ms. Allen taught, a former fellow teacher said, "With a lot of love." She cared about the children and they *perceived* that caring. Thus, many years later the students' perceptions of this teacher's concern had a direct and positive impact on their well being.

In a radically different setting, the chief executive officer of a company employing about three hundred people was experiencing unusual reactions from the union, which represented about one hundred of the employees. It seemed he was immune from attack or "demonization" even during tough contract negotiations. Regardless of what he did, the union did not attack him personally. Subsequently, he asked a former union leader why this was, and the man responded, "You care about the employees—and they know it." Without recognizing it, this CEO had been enhancing the perception of caring as a tool for managing.

Building a stronger foundation

This book is, above all, a book of optimism. We believe that once parents understand the perceptions they create in their children's minds, they are in a powerful position to change misperceptions—and to build a new perception of love.

By taking the simple tests provided here, parents can actually measure the amount of love their children are perceiving and identify areas that need improvement. Equally important, they can learn the skills needed to shore up those fundamentals of love: empathy, communication, and the five "W's."

Finally, parents can understand the way they communicate love and caring and discover ways to incorporate the twelve positive parenting styles into their relationships with their children.

Is this book a cure-all for the inevitable problems and difficulties that lie in the task of parenting? No. Parenting is undoubtedly one of the most challenging tasks on earth, and, because parents are human, mistakes are inevitable.

Does this book claim that there is only one "correct" approach to child-rearing? No. As unique individuals, parents must raise their children in accordance with their own beliefs, experiences, and values. Recently, a twelve-hour course was offered for fifty clergy and lay personnel attending a Christian counseling training center. The course taught pastoral counselors and those aspiring to such work to use the concepts, tests, and materials in this book. Following completion of the twelve-hour basic course, the students were supervised in working with fifty families using the perception of love concepts. The results were extraordinary.

Students of all ages participated in the course. Several reported that the course changed their lives in the way they dealt with others—in particular with their own *adult* children. The course caused them to examine how they had raised their children and to engage in dialogue with these now-grown children. These parents reported significant, positive change. Others reported immediate and positive change in dealing with adolescent children, and evaluation of the supervised field work provided anecdotal evidence of the way these methods increased communication. And all this occurred during the *developmental* phase of this approach.

What this book does claim is that parents can incorporate new knowledge and skills into their interactions with their children to increase their children's perception of the all-important love their parents feel for them.

We wish you much success as you begin to incorporate what you have learned from this book into your life. We encourage you to start small, to avoid discouragement, and to recognize that making changes takes time, patience, and persistence. But the rewards will be well worth the effort.

The fact that you have taken the time to read this book

speaks volumes about your love for your children. It is now up to you to build on that love to create a better, more wonderful relationship with your children—one in which they join the ranks of those fortunate children who know they are loved, and reap the benefits of that love for a lifetime.

APPENDIX

Chapters 7 and 8 contain tests to measure the perception of love in your family. Another complete set of these is included here for your use. Please refer to the appropriate chapters for scoring and analyses of the results.

Mother—For Preteen Child

1. Read each question carefully. There are 72 in all.
2. The questions require you to try to see things the way you think your child sees them. This is really tough because you are trying to visualize what you do as seen through the eyes of someone else—your child.
3. If you agree that the statement correctly describes the way you think your child would say you act *most of the time*, then check the "Yes" box.
4. If you think that your child believes you *do not* act that way *most of the time*, then check the "No" box.
5. The test is *only* about how you think that child sees you. Don't consider how your child sees anyone else or how anyone else sees you.
6. Do not discuss the answers with anyone while completing this test.

REMEMBER: DO YOU AGREE THAT THIS IS THE WAY YOUR CHILD *THINKS YOU ACT?*

1. Does your mother allow you to pick your own friends?
   Yes___ No___

2. Does your mother let you choose what you want to do whenever possible?
   Yes___ No___

3. Does your mother allow you to spend the money you earn in any way you pick?
   Yes___ No___

4. Does your mother let you plan your own schedule to do your chores?
   Yes___ No___

5. Does your mother let you decide what you will wear when you will be with your friends?
   Yes___ No___

6. Will your mother let you decide the colors to paint the walls of your bedroom?
   Yes___ No___

7. Does your mother enjoy having you bring your friends home?
   Yes___ No___

8. Does your mother let you have friends at home often?
   Yes___ No___

9. Do your friends respect your mother?
   Yes___ No___

10. Does your mother treat your friends with respect and courtesy?
    Yes___ No___

11. Does your mother include you in adult conversations with her friends and relatives?
    Yes___ No___

12. Does your mother try to meet your friends' parents?
    Yes___ No___

13. Can you tell your mother if you think your ideas are better than hers?
    Yes___ No___

14. Does your mother ask you how to do certain things?
    Yes___ No___

15. Does your mother like you to do things your own way?
    Yes___ No___

16. Does your mother prefer you to consider her ideas before making up your mind?
    Yes___ No___

17. Does your mother encourage you to both ask questions and to find answers?
    Yes___ No___

18. Does your mother encourage you to also consider unusual solutions to problems?
    Yes___ No___

19. Does your mother like to talk about things with you?
    Yes___ No___

20. Does your mother like for you to tease her occasionally about some things?
    Yes___ No___

21. Does your mother really want you to tell her about how you feel about things?
    Yes___ No___

22. Your mother doesn't talk down to you.
    Yes___ No___

23. Does your mother give you information to help make decisions but then won't order you around?
    Yes___ No___

24. Does your mother tease you as if you were an adult?
    Yes___ No___

25. Does your mother say that you are very good-natured?
    Yes___ No___

26. Is your mother happy to see you when you come home from school?
    Yes___ No___

27. Does your mother tell you that she's proud of you?
    Yes___ No___

28. Does your mother compliment you when you do something well?
    Yes___ No___

29. Does your mother speak more often of what you do well rather than of the mistakes you make?
    Yes___ No___

30. Does your mother often praise you in front of other people?
    Yes___ No___

31. Does your mother enjoy talking things over with you?
    Yes___ No___

32. Does your mother enjoy doing things with you?
    Yes___ No___

33. Does your mother have a good time at home with you?
    Yes___ No___

34. Has your mother talked about her problems and her successes with you?
    Yes___ No___

35. Does your mother talk about her childhood with you?
    Yes___ No___

36. Does your mother enjoy teaching you how to use some of her personal things?
    Yes___ No___

37. Does your mother mostly speak to you in a warm and friendly voice?
    Yes___ No___

38. Does your mother often smile at you?
    Yes___ No___

39. Does your mother tell you how much she loves you?
    Yes___ No___

40. Does your mother kiss you on the cheek when she comes home?
    Yes___ No___

41. Does your mother use warm and affectionate nicknames for you?
    Yes___ No___

42. Does your mother tell you how much she misses you when you are away from each other?
    Yes___ No___

43. Does your mother make you feel better if you talk over your worries with her?
    Yes___ No___

44. Does your mother give you sympathy when you need it?
    Yes___ No___

45. Does your mother cheer you up when you are sad?
    Yes___ No___

46. Does your mother encourage you to keep working at solving a tough problem?
    Yes___ No___

47. Does your mother try to help you understand that there are both good times and bad times in life?
    Yes___ No___

48. Does your mother listen when you need someone to listen to you?
    Yes___ No___

49. Does your mother encourage you to read?
    Yes___ No___

50. Does your mother help you find out more about things that are important to you?
    Yes___ No___

51. Does your mother talk with you about science?
    Yes___ No___

52. Does your mother help you to make things?
    Yes___ No___

53. Does your mother play games with you that make you think a lot?
    Yes___ No___

54. Does your mother encourage you to learn about computers?
    Yes___ No___

55. Does your mother often give up something to be able to get something for you?
    Yes___ No___

56. Does your mother make you feel like the most important person in her life?
    Yes___ No___

57. Does your mother give you a lot of care and attention?
    Yes___ No___

58. Does your mother do things with you that she knows you like doing?
    Yes___ No___

59. Is your mother concerned that you have a good time when you do things together?
    Yes___ No___

60. Does your mother consider your needs before her own?
    Yes___ No___

61. Does your mother like you to spend a lot of your free time at home?

    Yes____   No____

62. Does your mother seem to be sorry you are growing up?

    Yes____   No____

63. Does your mother allow you much time to yourself?

    Yes____   No____

64. Does your mother seem to feel hurt if you want to do things alone?

    Yes____   No____

65. Does your mother want you to be like her when she was in school?

    Yes____   No____

66. Does your mother want you to grow up to be just like her?

    Yes____   No____

67. Does your mother worry about your health?

    Yes____   No____

68. Does your mother worry that something might happen to you?

    Yes____   No____

69. Does your mother work hard to prevent you from failing at something you want to do?

    Yes____   No____

70. Is your mother concerned about your playing some sports because they could be dangerous?

    Yes____   No____

71. Is your mother very careful about the kinds of friends you choose?
    Yes___ No___

72. Does your mother make sure that you follow the rules and stay out of trouble?
    Yes___ No___

You have completed the test.

Father—For Preteen Child

1. Read each question carefully. There are 72 in all.
2. The questions require you to try to see things the way you think your child sees them. This is really tough because you are trying to visualize what you do as seen through the eyes of someone else—your child.
3. If you agree that the statement correctly describes the way you think your child would say you act *most of the time,* then check the "Yes" box.
4. If you think that your child believes you *do not* act that way *most of the time,* then check the "No" box.
5. The test is *only* about how you think that child sees you. Don't consider how your child sees anyone else or how anyone else sees you.
6. Do not discuss the answers with anyone while completing this test.

REMEMBER: DO YOU AGREE THAT THIS IS THE WAY YOUR CHILD *THINKS YOU ACT?*

1. Does your father allow you to pick your own friends?
    Yes___ No___

2. Does your father let you choose what you want to do whenever possible?
    Yes___ No___

3. Does your father allow you to spend the money you earn in any way you pick?
    Yes___ No___

4. Does your father let you plan your own schedule to do your chores?
    Yes___ No___

5. Does your father let you decide what you will wear when you will be with your friends?
    Yes___ No___

6. Will your father let you decide the colors to paint the walls of your bedroom?
    Yes___ No___

7. Does your father enjoy having you bring your friends home?
    Yes___ No___

8. Does your father let you have friends at home often?
    Yes___ No___

9. Do your friends respect your father?
    Yes___ No___

10. Does your father treat your friends with respect and courtesy?
    Yes___ No___

11. Does your father include you in adult conversations with his friends and relatives?
    Yes___ No___

12. Does your father try to meet your friends' parents?
    Yes___ No___

13. Can you tell your father if you think your ideas are better than his?
    Yes___ No___

14. Does your father ask you how to do certain things?
    Yes___ No___

15. Does your father like you to do things your own way?
    Yes____ No____

16. Does your father prefer you to consider his ideas before making up your mind?
    Yes____ No____

17. Does your father encourage you to both ask questions and to find answers?
    Yes____ No____

18. Does your father encourage you to also consider unusual solutions to problems?
    Yes____ No____

19. Does your father like to talk about things with you?
    Yes____ No____

20. Does your father like for you to tease him occasionally about some things?
    Yes____ No____

21. Does your father really want you to tell him about how you feel about things?
    Yes____ No____

22. Your father doesn't talk down to you.
    Yes____ No____

23. Does your father give you information to help make decisions but then won't order you around?
    Yes____ No____

24. Does your father tease you as if you were an adult?
    Yes____ No____

25. Does your father say that you are very good-natured?
Yes___ No___

26. Does your father often praise you?
Yes___ No___

27. Does your father tell you that he's proud of you?
Yes___ No___

28. Does your father compliment you when you do something well?
Yes___ No___

29. Does your father speak more often of what you do well rather than of the mistakes you make?
Yes___ No___

30. Does your father often praise you in front of other people?
Yes___ No___

31. Does your father enjoy talking things over with you?
Yes___ No___

32. Does your father enjoy doing things with you?
Yes___ No___

33. Does your father have a good time at home with you?
Yes___ No___

34. Has your father talked about his problems and his successes with you?
Yes___ No___

35. Does your father talk about his childhood with you?
Yes___ No___

36. Does your father enjoy teaching you how to use some of his personal things?
    Yes___   No___

37. Does your father mostly speak to you in a warm and friendly voice?
    Yes___   No___

38. Does your father often smile at you?
    Yes___   No___

39. Does your father tell you that he loves you?
    Yes___   No___

40. Does your father embrace or hug you when he comes home?
    Yes___   No___

41. Does your father use warm and affectionate nicknames for you?
    Yes___   No___

42. Does your father tell you how much he misses you when you are away from each other?
    Yes___   No___

43. Does your father make you feel better if you talk over your worries with him?
    Yes___   No___

44. Does your father give you sympathy when you need it?
    Yes___   No___

45. Does your father cheer you up when you are sad?
    Yes___   No___

46. Does your father encourage you to keep working at solving a tough problem?
    Yes___   No___

47. Does your father try to help you understand that there are both good times and bad times in life?
    Yes___ No___

48. Does your father listen when you need someone to listen to you?
    Yes___ No___

49. Does your father encourage you to read?
    Yes___ No___

50. Does your father help you find out more about things that are important to you?
    Yes___ No___

51. Does your father talk with you about science?
    Yes___ No___

52. Does your father help you to make things?
    Yes___ No___

53. Does your father play games with you that make you think a lot?
    Yes___ No___

54. Does your father encourage you to learn about computers?
    Yes___ No___

55. Does your father often give up something to be able to get something for you?
    Yes___ No___

56. Does your father make you feel like the most important person in his life?
    Yes___ No___

57. Does your father give you a lot of care and attention?
    Yes___ No___

58. Does your father do things with you that he knows you like doing?
    Yes___ No___

59. Is your father concerned that you have a good time when you do things together?
    Yes___ No___

60. Does your father consider your needs before his own?
    Yes___ No___

61. Does your father like you to spend a lot of your free time at home?
    Yes___ No___

62. Does your father seem to be sorry you are growing up?
    Yes___ No___

63. Does your father allow you much time to yourself?
    Yes___ No___

64. Does your father seem to feel hurt if you want to do things alone?
    Yes___ No___

65. Does your father want you to be like him when he was in school?
    Yes___ No___

66. Does your father want you to grow up to be just like him?
    Yes___ No___

67. Does your father worry about your health?
    Yes___ No___

68. Does your father worry that something might happen to you?
    Yes___ No___

69. Does your father work hard to prevent you from failing at something you want to do?
    Yes___ No___

70. Is your father concerned about your playing some sports because they could be dangerous?
    Yes___ No___

71. Is your father very careful about the kinds of friends you choose?
    Yes___ No___

72. Does your father make sure that you follow the rules and stay out of trouble?
    Yes___ No___

You have completed the test.

Adolescent Tests—Chapter 8

ADOLESCENTS (ABOUT MOTHERS)

1. Read each question carefully. There are 72 in all.
2. If you agree that the statement correctly describes the way you think your Mother acts *most of the time* toward you, then check the "Yes" box.
3. If you think that your mother *does not* act that way *most of the time,* then check the "No" box.
4. The test is *only* about how you think your mother acts toward you. Don't consider how your mother acts toward anyone else or how anyone else acts toward you.
5. Do not discuss the answers with anyone while completing this test.

REMEMBER: DO YOU AGREE THAT THIS IS THE WAY YOU BELIEVE YOUR MOTHER ACTS TOWARD YOU?

1. Does your mother allow you to pick your own friends?
   Yes __   No __

2. Does your mother let you choose what you want to do whenever possible?
   Yes __   No __

3. Does your mother allow you to spend the money you earn in any way you pick?
   Yes __   No __

4. Does your mother let you plan your own schedule to do your chores?
   Yes __   No __

5. Does your mother let you decide what you will wear when you will be with your friends?
   Yes __   No __

6. Will your mother let you decide the colors to paint the walls of your bedroom?
   Yes __   No __

7. Does your mother enjoy having you bring your friends home?
   Yes __   No __

8. Does your mother let you have friends at home often?
   Yes __   No __

9. Do your friends respect your mother?
   Yes __   No __

10. Does your mother treat your friends with respect and courtesy?
    Yes __   No __

11. Does your mother include you in adult conversations with her friends and relatives?
Yes __   No __

12. Does your mother try to meet your friends' parents?
Yes __   No __

13. Can you tell your mother if you think your ideas are better than hers?
Yes __   No __

14. Does your mother ask you how to do certain things?
Yes __   No __

15. Does your mother like you to do things your own way?
Yes __   No __

16. Does your mother prefer you to consider her ideas before making up your mind?
Yes __   No __

17. Does your mother encourage you to both ask questions and to find answers?
Yes __   No __

18. Does your mother encourage you to also consider unusual solutions to problems?
Yes __   No __

19. Does your mother like to talk about things with you?
Yes __   No __

20. Does your mother like for you to tease her occasionally about some things?
Yes __   No __

21. Does your mother really want you to tell her about how you feel about things?
    Yes ___ No ___

22. Your mother doesn't talk down to you.
    Yes ___ No ___

23. Does your mother give you information to help make decisions but then won't order you around?
    Yes ___ No ___

24. Does your mother tease you as if you were an adult?
    Yes ___ No ___

25. Does your mother say that you are very good-natured?
    Yes ___ No ___

26. Is your mother happy to see you when you come home from school?
    Yes ___ No ___

27. Does your mother tell you that she's proud of you?
    Yes ___ No ___

28. Does your mother compliment you when you do something well?
    Yes ___ No ___

29. Does your mother speak more often of what you do well rather than the mistakes you make?
    Yes ___ No ___

30. Does your mother often praise you in front of other people?
    Yes ___ No ___

31. Does your mother enjoy talking things over with you?
    Yes ___ No ___

32. Does your mother enjoy doing things with you?
    Yes __ No __

33. Does your mother have a good time at home with you?
    Yes __ No __

34. Has your mother talked about her problems and her successes with you?
    Yes __ No __

35. Does your mother talk about her childhood with you?
    Yes __ No __

36. Does your mother enjoy teaching you how to use some of her personal things?
    Yes __ No __

37. Does your mother mostly speak to you in a warm and friendly voice?
    Yes __ No __

38. Does your mother often smile at you?
    Yes __ No __

39. Does your mother tell you how much she loves you?
    Yes __ No __

40. Does your mother kiss you on the cheek when she comes home?
    Yes __ No __

41. Does your mother use warm and affectionate nicknames for you?
    Yes __ No __

42. Does your mother tell you how much she misses you when you are away from each other?
    Yes __ No __

43. Does your mother make you feel better if you talk over your worries with her?
    Yes __ No __

44. Does your mother give you sympathy when you need it?
    Yes __ No __

45. Does your mother cheer you up when you are sad?
    Yes __ No __

46. Does your mother encourage you to keep working at solving a tough problem?
    Yes __ No __

47. Does your mother try to help you understand that there are both good times and bad times in life?
    Yes __ No __

48. Does your mother listen when you need someone to listen to you?
    Yes __ No __

49. Does your mother encourage you to read?
    Yes __ No __

50. Does your mother help you find out more about things that are important to you?
    Yes __ No __

51. Does your mother talk with you about science?
    Yes __ No __

52. Does your mother help you to make things?
    Yes __ No __

53. Does your mother play games with you that make you think a lot?
    Yes __ No __

54. Does your mother encourage you to learn about computers?
    Yes __ No __

55. Does your mother often give up something to be able to get something for you?
    Yes __ No __

56. Does your mother make you feel like the most important person in her life?
    Yes __ No __

57. Does your mother give you a lot of care and attention?
    Yes __ No __

58. Does your mother do things with you that she knows you like doing?
    Yes __ No __

59. Is your mother concerned that you have a good time when you do things together?
    Yes __ No __

60. Does your mother consider your needs before her own?
    Yes __ No __

61. Does your mother like you to spend a lot of your free time at home?
    Yes __ No __

62. Does your mother seem to be sorry you are growing up?
    Yes __ No __

63. Does your mother allow you much time to yourself?
    Yes __ No __

64. Does your mother seem to feel hurt if you want to do things alone?
    Yes __ No __

65. Does your mother want you to be like her when she was in school?

    Yes __   No __

66. Does your mother want you to grow up to be just like her?

    Yes __   No __

67. Does your mother worry about your health?

    Yes __   No __

68. Does your mother worry that something might happen to you?

    Yes __   No __

69. Does your mother work hard to prevent you from failing at something you want to do?

    Yes __   No __

70. Is your mother concerned about your playing some sports because they could be dangerous?

    Yes __   No __

71. Is your mother very careful about the kinds of friends you choose?

    Yes __   No __

72. Does your mother make sure that you follow the rules and stay out of trouble?

    Yes __   No __

You have completed the test.

ADOLESCENTS (ABOUT FATHERS)

1. Read each question carefully. There are 72 in all.
2. If you agree that the statement correctly describes the way you think your father acts *most of the time* toward you, then check the "Yes" box.
3. If you think that your father *does not* act that way *most of the time,* then check the "No" box.
4. The test is *only* about how you think your father acts toward you. Don't consider how your father acts toward anyone else or how anyone else acts toward you.
5. Do not discuss the answers with anyone while completing this test.

REMEMBER: DO YOU AGREE THAT THIS IS THE WAY YOU BELIEVE YOUR FATHER ACTS TOWARD YOU?

1. Does your father allow you to pick your own friends?
   Yes __ No __

2. Does your father let you choose what you want to do whenever possible?
   Yes __ No __

3. Does your father allow you to spend the money you earn in any way you pick?
   Yes __ No __

4. Does your father let you plan your own schedule to do your chores?
   Yes __ No __

5. Does your father let you decide what you will wear when you will be with your friends?
   Yes __ No __

6. Will your father let you decide the colors to paint the walls of your bedroom?
   Yes __ No __

7. Does your father enjoy having you bring your friends home?
   Yes __ No __

8. Does your father let you have friends at home often?
   Yes __ No __

9. Do your friends respect your father?
   Yes __ No __

10. Does your father treat your friends with respect and courtesy?
    Yes __ No __

11. Does your father include you in adult conversations with his friends and relatives?
    Yes __ No __

12. Does your father try to meet your friends' parents?
    Yes __ No __

13. Can you tell your father if you think your ideas are better than his?
    Yes __ No __

14. Does your father ask you how to do certain things?
    Yes __ No __

15. Does your father like you to do things your own way?
    Yes __ No __

16. Does your father prefer you to consider his ideas before making up your mind?
    Yes __ No __

17. Does your father encourage you to both ask questions and to find answers?
    Yes __ No __

18. Does your father encourage you to also consider unusual solutions to problems?
    Yes __ No

19. Does your father like to talk about things with you?
    Yes __ No __

20. Does your father like for you to tease him occasionally about some things?
    Yes __ No __

21. Does your father really want you to tell him about how you feel about things?
    Yes __ No __

22. Your father doesn't talk down to you.
    Yes __ No __

23. Does your father give you information to help make decisions but then won't order you around?
    Yes __ No __

24. Does your father tease you as if you were an adult?
    Yes __ No __

25. Does your father say that you are very good-natured?
    Yes __ No __

26. Does your father often praise you?
    Yes __ No __

27. Does your father tell you that he's proud of you?
    Yes __ No __

28. Does your father compliment you when you do something well?
    Yes __ No __

29. Does your father speak more often of what you do well rather than of the mistakes you make?
    Yes __ No __

30. Does your father often praise you in front of other people?
    Yes __ No __

31. Does your father enjoy talking things over with you?
    Yes __ No __

32. Does your father enjoy doing things with you?
    Yes __ No __

33. Does your father have a good time at home with you?
    Yes __ No __

34. Has your father talked about his problems and his successes with you?
    Yes __ No __

35. Does your father talk about his childhood with you?
    Yes __ No __

36. Does your father enjoy teaching you how to use some of his personal things?
    Yes __ No __

37. Does your father mostly speak to you in a warm and friendly voice?
    Yes __ No __

38. Does your father often smile at you?
    Yes __ No __

39. Does your father tell you how much he loves you?
    Yes __ No __

40. Does your father embrace or hug you when he comes home?
    Yes __ No __

41. Does your father use warm and affectionate nicknames for you?
    Yes __ No __

42. Does your father tell you how much he misses you when you are away from each other?
    Yes __ No __

43. Does your father make you feel better if you talk over your worries with him?
    Yes __ No __

44. Does your father give you sympathy when you need it?
    Yes __ No __

45. Does your father cheer you up when you are sad?
    Yes __ No __

46. Does your father encourage you to keep working at solving a tough problem?
    Yes __ No __

47. Does your father try to help you understand that there are both good times and bad times in life?
    Yes __ No __

48. Does your father listen when you need someone to listen to you?
    Yes __ No __

49. Does your father encourage you to read?
    Yes __ No __

50. Does your father help you find out more about things that are important to you?
    Yes __ No __

51. Does your father talk with you about science?
    Yes __ No __

52. Does your father help you to make things?
    Yes __ No __

53. Does your father play games with you that make you think a lot?
    Yes __ No __

54. Does your father encourage you to learn about computers?
    Yes __ No __

55. Does your father often give up something to be able to get something for you?
    Yes __ No __

56. Does your father make you feel like the most important person in his life?
    Yes __ No __

57. Does your father give you a lot of care and attention?
    Yes __ No __

58. Does your father do things with you that he knows you like doing?
    Yes __ No __

59. Is your father concerned that you have a good time when you do things together?
    Yes __ No __

60. Does your father consider your needs before his own?
    Yes __   No __

61. Does your father like you to spend a lot of your free time at home?
    Yes __   No __

62. Does your father seem to be sorry you are growing up?
    Yes __   No __

63. Does your father allow you much time to yourself?
    Yes __   No __

64. Does your father seem to feel hurt if you want to do things alone?
    Yes __   No __

65. Does your father want you to be like him when he was in school?
    Yes __   No __

66. Does your father want you to grow up to be just like him?
    Yes __   No __

67. Does your father worry about your health?
    Yes __   No __

68. Does your father worry that something might happen to you?
    Yes __   No __

69. Does your father work hard to prevent you from failing at something you want to do?
    Yes __   No __

70. Is your father concerned about your playing some sports because they could be dangerous?
    Yes __   No __

71. Is your father very careful about the kinds of friends you choose?

    Yes __ No __

72. Does your father make sure that you follow the rules and stay out of trouble?

    Yes __ No __

You have completed the test.

Special Offer

This book contains tests to measure and analyze the child's perception of love. There are sufficient tests and analysis forms included to cover the perceptions of love for:

- a mother and one adolescent child,
- a father and one adolescent child,
- a mother and one pre-adolescent child,
- a father and one pre-adolescent child.

For larger families or for retesting in the future, we suggest ordering our Compact Disc for a Windows computer. This disc and system allows you to retest on a regular schedule as often as you like. You may also use it for all combinations of parents and children in the family. Therapists, counselors, and others who are providing help to families using Do Your Kids Know You Love Them? may use the disc (tests and analyses) for each of the families. The results of the scoring can be printed out and saved.

Compact Disc—Perception of Love **(For Windows computers ONLY)**
Price: $9.95 each, plus $2.05 shipping and handling (includes sales tax)

Number of discs ordered: _____   @ $12.00_____
Shipping & handling included
                                         Total   _____   _____

Method of Payment

Please charge my VISA or Mastercard Account for the Total shown above.

Account No. _____ _____ _____ _____ Exp. Date: _____

To order, complete this order form and send it with the credit card information to **Peoplescience, Inc. 20 Pine Valley Lane, Monroe Twp, NJ 08831**

Ship the disc to:
Name: _____
Street Address: _____ Apt. No. _____
City or Town: _____
State & Zip: _____

Tel. No. Area code: _____ phone number: _____